are the christadelphians a cult?

are the christadelphians a cult?

p. craig bresych

NEW COVENANT PRESS

ARE THE CHRISTADELPHIANS A CULT?
Copyright © 2022 New Covenant Press and P. Craig Bresych

New Covenant Press
Unit 90616
Courier Point
13 Freeland Park
Wareham Road
Poole, Dorset
BH16 6FH
United Kingdom

Front cover art credits: © Michael Halbert
Cover and book design: Philip P. Kapusta
Typeset in 11 point Minion Pro (Adobe Systems).
This paper is acid free and lignin free. It meets all ANSI standards for archival quality paper.

Library of Congress Control Number: 2022922268
International Standard Book Number: 979-8-3663969-2-9

Publisher's Cataloging-in-Publication Data

Bresych, P. Craig, 1960 —
    Are the Christadelphians a cult? / P. Craig Bresych.
    p.   cm.
    ISBN-13: 979-8-3663969-2-9 (pbk.: alk. paper)

                                                    2022922268

Then they said to him,
"Say 'Shibboleth!'"
If he said,
"Sibboleth"
(and could not pronounce the word correctly),
they grabbed him and executed him
right there at the fords of the Jordan.
On that day forty-two thousand
Ephraimites fell
dead.

Judges 12:6 (NET)

Contents

CHAPTER 1

The Most Ambivalent Monosyllable

There was much murmuring among the people concerning him [Jesus]: for some said, He is a good man:
others said, Nay; but he deceiveth the people.

—JOHN 7:12

As a christian you should be defending the gospel of
Jesus Christ, God and the word of God. If you find
yourself defending the church, bishop or the pastor
you are not attending the church, but you are doing a
cult.[1]

—DJ KYOS

FOR CENTURIES, THE meaning of the word *cult* was limited in
scope and without controversy. This is no longer the case. Today,
the word *cult* has come to mean so many things that the word has
lost its usefulness. On one side of the spectrum, a cult is seen as something radical, pejorative, involving fanatical, blind enthusiasm and collective mystical delusion. In these instances, the use of the word often
(but not always) involves a charismatic personality who has (or once
had) great influence over the beliefs and actions of those who are drawn
towards and associate with such an individual. But on the other side of
the spectrum, the word has become little more than a way to describe an
enthusiast or an ardent admirer of trendy products. And in the middle,
the word is used as a label to ostracize those who hold minority opinions
by those who are in the majority.

It is here, in the middle, where we encounter a more serious problem, for it has become common for mainstream Christians to label the

---

1. Kyos Magupe, https://www.djkyos.com.

adherents of minority Christian groups as belonging to a cult when a core doctrine held by the latter differs significantly from the former. In many of these cases a more accurate term to use when describing such groups is the word *sect*, at least within English-speaking North America.[2] Here, within the context of religion, a *sect* is a group of people characterized by one or more doctrines which are typically considered nonconforming by the larger religious community to which they belong.

In the early days of Christianity, the opponents of Jesus and his followers described the new Christian faith as a sect,[3] not as a cult, even though at the heart of this new movement was a charismatic leader, many new teachings, enthusiastic followers, and a threat to an established religion—all characteristics of what today defines a "cult" in the minds of many people. Yet despite qualifying as a cult based on these modern identifiers, the new "Jesus-cult" was described in its time by its adversaries in this manner:

> But we desire to hear from you what your views are; for with regard to this sect we know that everywhere it is spoken against. (Acts 28:22, RSV)

In the Greek, the word rendered here *sect* is αιρεσεως (hah'-ee-res-is),[4] a noun which is derived from the verb αἱρέομαι (hahee-reh'-om-ahee), meaning *to make a choice, to choose,* or *to prefer.* The original meaning of *cult,* on the other hand, is not as simple to explain. As we will see, although it once had a clear and limited meaning, it no longer does.

---

2. One exception is in Europe, where the word *sect* can have the same pejorative connotation that the word *cult* now has in North America.

3. Nearly all English translations of Acts 28:22 use the word *sect*, with the few exceptions choosing the phrase "form of religion" (Bible in Basic English) or the term "movement" (New Living Translation).

4. From which we get the words *heresy* and *heretic.* Like the word *cult*, the word *heresy* has morphed from its original meaning. One can see this when comparing the King James translation with modern translations of the Bible (cf. Acts 24:14, 1 Corinthians 11:19, Galatians 5:20). Today *heresy* has a sinister connotation, but in the 17th century, *heresy* meant the same thing as a *faction* or *clique.*

A Look Back at Cult-ure

In the 17th century, the English word *cult* had a narrow application. It was used to describe "a *particular form* or *system* of worship."[5] It derived from the French word *culte*, which itself is derived from Latin *cultus,* meaning, "care, labor; cultivation, culture; worship, reverence."[6] *Cult* was literally the "care" owed to deities and to temples, shrines, or churches.

For example, in the specific context of the Greek hero cult, archaeologist and Duke University professor of Classical studies Carla Antonaccio wrote:

> The term *cult* identifies a pattern of ritual behavior in connection with specific objects, within a framework of spatial and temporal coordinates. *Ritual* behavior would include (but not necessarily be limited to) prayer, sacrifice, votive offerings, competitions, processions and construction of monuments. Some degree of both recurrence in place and repetition over time of ritual action is necessary for a cult to be enacted, to be practiced.[7]

In the Catholic Church, the Latin *cultus* is the technical term for Roman Catholic devotions or veneration extended to a particular saint.

From the Latin word *cultus,* we also get the word *culture,* meaning the core system of beliefs, activities, and traits of a social group. Thus, every human being belongs to a cult in its most general sense, because everyone belongs to a culture which is conveyed by the language they speak and the habits they have formed.

In the 18th century, however, the word *cult* was rarely used outside of the context of ancient Greco-Roman and Ancient Near East worship. The word did not even appear in Samuel Johnson's 1755 *Dictionary of the English Language.* But the word does appear in our dictionaries today. For example, *Webster's Dictionary* includes this definition of *cult:*

---

5. "Cult," *Online Etymology Dictionary,* https://www.etymonline.com/search?q=cult (accessed August 30, 2022), with emphasis added.

6. Ibid.

7. Carla M. Antonaccio, "Contesting the Past: Hero Cult, Tomb Cult, and Epic in Early Greece," *American Journal of Archaeology,* vol. 98, no. 3 (July 1994), p. 398.

"A system of religious worship or ritual, devoted attachment to, or extravagant admiration for, a person, principle, etc."[8]

The meaning of the term significantly morphed in the 20th century. Today, in many cases, the word *cult* is used as a highly pejorative label, applied to any cohesive religious group which the surrounding religious establishment considers outside the mainstream or possibly dangerous in some sense.

This change in meaning is partly the result of the rise and fall of headline-grabbing religious groups known for mass suicide and murder to which governments and news media in the U.S. have applied the label *cult*. Charges of mind control, economic and sexual exploitation, and other forms of abuse were routinely levied against these groups. Beginning in 1978, when over 900 people died in Jonestown, Guyana, under the control of Reverend Jim Jones, the public imagination has been captured by several similar events which have reshaped the meaning of the word. The tragedies and crimes associated with the Peoples Temple at Jonestown, the Branch Davidians,[9] the Order of the Solar Temple,[10] Aum Shinrikyo[11] and Heaven's Gate[12] have contributed to the re-framing of the term. As a result, the word *cult* now carries with it significant negative and sinister connotations.

---

8. *Webster's New World Dictionary of the American Language*, College Edition (New York: The World Publishing Company, 1957), p. 358.

9. The Branch Davidians were an apocalyptic new religious movement associated with the Seventh-Day Adventists and was founded in 1955. They and their leader, David Koresh, made headlines in 1993 when U.S. federal agents raided their compound in Waco, Texas, after a 51-day standoff. Seventy-six members, many of them children, along with Koresh, died in a fire that erupted during the siege.

10. Starting in 1994, a group known as the Order of the Solar Temple was associated with a series of murders and mass suicides that claimed several dozen lives in France, Switzerland, and Canada. Articles from *The New York Times* covering the events had headlines such as "Murder Is Suspected in Cult Deaths in France," "Swiss Authorities Seek Cult's 2 Top Leaders on Homicide Charges in Followers' Deaths," and "A Secret and Charismatic Cult Leader".

11. A Japanese doomsday cult founded in 1987. It carried out the deadly Tokyo subway sarin attack in 1995 and was found to have been responsible for the Matsumoto sarin attack the previous year.

12. An American religious movement founded in 1974 that taught a mixture of Christian millenarianism, New Age, and what one might call a UFO spaceship religion. On March 26, 1997, the bodies of the 39 active members of the group were found in a house in a suburb of San Diego. They had participated in a mass suicide coinciding with the closest approach of Comet Hale–Bopp.

Time magazine cover for April 3, 1995 featuring Shoko Asahara, the founder of Aum Shinrikyo, a Japanese doomsday cult founded in 1987. It carried out the deadly Tokyo subway sarin attack in 1995 and was found to have been responsible for the Matsumoto sarin attack the previous year.

★★★★
FINAL

DAILY ⊚ NEWS

Sunny, cold, 40s.
Cloudy and cold
tomorrow. Near 46.
Details page 83.

Vol. 60. No. 51   New York, Monday, November 20, 1978   Price: 20 cents

MASS SUICIDES IN GUYANA CULT

Report 300 dead found at site

NBC-TV newsman Don Harris (left) and photographer Greg Robinson (right) are shown in film taken by NBC cameraman Robert Brown moments before they and Rep. Leo Ryan (D-Calif.) were shot to death in Guyana.   —*Stories on page 3; other pictures in centerfold*

JOAN CRAWFORD | **THE PRIVATE PICTURE OF A MOTHER**
New series starts today
Pages 38 and 39

On November 18, 1978, Peoples Temple founder Jim Jones led hundreds of his followers in a mass murder-suicide at their agricultural commune in a remote part of the South American nation of Guyana. Many of Jones' followers willingly ingested a poison-laced punch while others were forced to do so at gunpoint. The final death toll at the Jonestown compound that day was 909; a third of those who perished were children.

The Ambiguous, Ambivalent Cult

According to *Merriam-Webster's Dictionary*, the word *cult* can now be broadly defined as any of the following:

- formal religious veneration
- a system of religious beliefs and its body of adherents
- a religion regarded as unorthodox or spurious
- great devotion to a person, idea, object or movement
- a group united by devotion or allegiance to an artistic or intellectual movement or figure

Unfortunately, the last definition makes it possible for everyone from Barbie doll collectors to die-hard Elvis fans to be labeled as belonging to a cult. As one modern commentator recognized, "Given its connotative breadth, it [the word cult] may be the most ambivalent monosyllable in the language."[13] Citing recent examples, he wrote:

Did you enjoy Elizabeth Moss' character in *Mad Men*? Then you were involved, however briefly, in the Cult of Peggy. In March, Slate critiqued the "cult of Steve Jobs." In April, the *Washington Post* investigated the "cult of the Ph.D." In June, Richard Brody urged readers of the *New Yorker* to "free yoursel[ves] from the cult of Marlon Brando," while Business Insider was busy rending its garments over the demise of the "cult of Lululemon." In July, *Pacific Standard* contributor Alana Massey wrote in Hazlitt against the "cult of work"—a lament not unlike Dina Kaplan's "The Cult of Busy" in Medium. Recently, the *Columbia Journalism Review* published a report by Chris Ip on the "cult" of Vice magazine, while Politico has identified the "Cult of Neil deGrasse Tyson" and the "Cult of Calhoun."[14]

---

13. Ted Scheinman, "Cult Week," *Pacific Standard*, https://psmag.com/series/cult-week (accessed February 15, 2019).
14. Ibid.

Christianity: A First Century Cult?

The Christianity of the first century started out as a small group in high tension with the surrounding society, posing a threat to the prevailing, dominant religions, be it paganism or Judaism. When Christianity began, it was a minority system consisting of unique beliefs and controversial practices such as holy communion. When it was a small, minority group within the Roman Empire, it was often criticized by those who did not understand it or who were threatened by changes its adoption might bring. Christians were branded as unpatriotic because they refused to honor the state deities and viewed as anti-social because they did not participate in the forms of entertainment and behavior common to the rest of society. Rumors were spread by detractors about Christians drinking human blood and eating human flesh. However, when it became an official state religion, endorsed and sponsored by generals and emperors of Rome and widely accepted by the citizenry, Christianity's practices informed the activities of the culture as a whole. Interestingly, when a new religion becomes large or dominant in a society, the cult then becomes *culture*.

Yet, in 21st century Christian parlance, referring to a new religious movement's status as a "cult" is something akin to calling a group "a bunch of dangerous fanatics" or "brainwashed religious zealots." It is a pejorative label, representing a type of in-group/out-group terminology designed to quickly condemn and communicate exclusion. Its use is a convenient way to quickly dismiss another group, and is typically based on underlying fear, prejudice, or bias resulting from a lack of understanding or careful examination of the group to which the label is applied. This mostly emotional, reactionary bias is confirmed by the fact that scholars, academics, and sociologists avoid the use of the term when describing new or relatively new religious groups.[15] This bias is something that I can personally attest to.

---

15. In 1999, the Maryland State Task Force to Study the Effects of Cult Activities on Public Senior [sic] Higher Education Institutions admitted in its final report that it had "decided not to attempt to define the world 'cult'" and proceeded to avoid the word entirely in its final report, except in its title and introduction. https://www.cesnur.org/testi/maryland_rpt.htm (accessed July 22, 2022).

A Personal Story

In 1985, I stumbled across a small advertisement in my local newspaper. It was nothing more than a phone number with a heading. Call the phone number if you wished to listen to a minute-long prerecorded message on various Bible topics, was the gist. My curiosity piqued, I dialed, and listened. At the end of the recording, the kind voice generously offered to send me more information, for free, on the topic if I left my name and mailing address. And so I did.

What I received in the mail was an introduction letter and a booklet on the topic of eternal life. The letter was from a group that I had never heard of before: the Christadelphians. This was pre-Internet, pre-Google, and if I wanted to learn more about this unknown group I had to do my research the hard way: I had to actually read what they sent me.

Truth be told, I didn't like what I read. What I encountered was not what I had been taught growing up in church or on the Christian radio stations. Eternal life existed on earth, not in heaven. Immortal souls and eternal torments for the damned in hell were fables, the booklet claimed. Looking back, I could have easily just thrown the stuff in the trash and moved on, but instead, I decided to investigate the group. Clearly they were in error, and perhaps it was my Christian duty to convert one of them to "orthodoxy" one day, should I ever encounter a Christadelphian in the flesh.

Back in those days I had easy access to the Library of Congress in Washington, DC, so I decided I'd start my investigation there. I entered the Jefferson Room and was greeted at the door by a librarian. She greeted me politely and asked if she could be of any assistance. This being my first visit to the Library of Congress, I quickly accepted her assistance. I said, "Yes, I am doing research on a Christian cult." The librarian responded, "Which one?" I replied, "The Christadelphians," and then helped her with its spelling. After a minute of typing and perusing over her primitive computer terminal, she replied, "Sir, the Christadelphians are not a cult. They're a sect." And so with this correction humbly accepted, I began what would become a study of the Christadelphians lasting nearly four decades. This book is the product of that investigation.

I did not intend to write a book on the Christadelphians when I first started on this journey nearly forty years ago. Nor did I have such a desire even two years ago. What motivated me to eventually compile this book were the repeated encounters of unfair treatment of the Christadelphians by other Christians.

One such example comes from a news article in a newspaper called *Christian Today*.[16] According to their website, *Christian Today* strives to become the number one news source for Christians in Australia, a source of "extensive and up-to-date coverage on the latest Christian events or news."

The article that I stumbled across a few years ago was written by a reporter who had recently moved to Brisbane, and it described her search for a new church in her new neighborhood. The author shared how:

> When moving into my new place last week, it was a shock for me to discover a cult living just up the road. The shock wasn't the fact that it was a cult in the third largest city in the country—that's to be expected. The shock was that I had never heard of them!

> I was walking around the neighbourhood, trying to find a nice church to get involved with when lo and behold, I came across a rather humble building of Christadelphians. At first I thought: 'this looks like a nice church, anything with the word Christ in it has to be good, right?' but soon I found my assumptions to be sorely mistaken.[17]

The title of the news article was "Cult truth vs. orthodoxy," and the "reporter" made it clear that she wasn't interested in anything other than what she called "orthodoxy":

> Being orthodox is the safe way. Because there is so much deception out there and frankly when people harp on about a

---

16. Not to be confused with the better-known periodical *Christianity Today*.
17. Bridget Brenton, "Cult truth vs. orthodoxy," *Christian Today*, January 15, 2013, http://christiantoday.com.au/news/cult-truth-vs-orthodoxy.html (accessed September 5, 2022).

certain doctrine it gets on my last nerve. I no longer fruitlessly debate theology but I take my stand on the orthodox position of Jesus as the Son of God, as God Himself [...]

I take the orthodox position so I can tell when anyone is trying to preach another Jesus to me. So I don't unthinkingly wander into some 'church' like the Christadelphians and start drinking in everything they say like the fruit punch in Jonestown.

Be orthodox but not more orthodox than the others[18]

Orthodoxy keeps you on your guard.[19]

It is a remarkable piece on many counts. What struck me most was that this "reporter" made no mention of actually meeting the Christadelphians in the "humble building" that she came across. Her words give the reader the impression that she never even set a foot in the "Christadelphian church," let alone talk to any Christadelphians prior to writing the article. If my supposition is true, this means that her conclusion that the Christadelphians are a cult was most likely the result of her going online and performing a web search for "Christadelphians" and finding less than positive things written about them. I won't begrudge her for using the Internet to do her research if this is what she did. I do it regularly. We all do it. But what bothers me is the thought that a reporter could fail to report the other side of the story. Was she so fearful of "drinking the fruit punch in Jonestown" that she passed off shallow and jaundiced information as if it were fact? Can a reporter not bother to venture a foot into "a rather humble building of Christadelphians" in Brisbane to ask a single question and then share the response with her readers? Did such supposed lack of research lead her to conclude that the Christadelphians were in the same category as the followers of Jim Jones? Whatever she did or didn't do, it is clear she felt it was her Christian duty to warn her fellow Australians (and others worldwide) to stay away from this "cult" and to take shelter in the arms of "orthodoxy." The

---

18. Original heading.
19. Ibid.

article did not come across to me as impartial news reporting, regardless of my religious background.

The wholesale dismissal of the Christadelphians based upon a quick online search is bound to be a common occurrence these days. And truth be told, perhaps I would have done exactly the same thing when I first encountered this particular faith group nearly forty years ago (assuming the worldwide web had been available in the early 1980s). But the difference between this Australian reporter and myself is that I will be sharing the Christadelphian side of the story with the reader and will allow you to decide for yourself whether the Christadelphians are a cult or not. You can also decide for yourself whether "orthodoxy" is a comfortable place to take shelter. I have learned the hard way that listening to only one side of a story is not the way for anyone, professional reporter or not, to seek after truth.

Therefore, what you will find in this book, unlike the Australian article, is an in-depth look at this group called the Christadelphians. It is the result of decades of research and discussion with the Christadelphians. It is the result of stepping into their buildings, talking to them in person, critically examining their literature, thoroughly researching their history, searching for skeletons in closets, and debating with them in person and on paper. Perhaps critics will say that I drank the "fruit punch" by doing these things. Of course it is a risk. But if we are to treat others as we would want to be treated ourselves, we must go beyond a thirty minute engagement with an online search engine. To fairly answer the question, "Are the Christadelphians a cult?" we must be willing to take the time to consider more than one side of the story.

CHAPTER 2

Characteristics of a Cult

> The quickest way to detect a cult is to sniff for doublethink. The cult seeks control over its membership not by providing a coherent theological system but by providing the opposite: an unstable theology infinitely malleable to the needs of the cult's top echelon and uninterpretable at all times to anyone below that level.[1]
>
> —BENJAMIN WITTES

A S SET FORTH in the first chapter, today's concept of a cult has been cut loose from its original entomological moorings. No longer does the term simply mean *a system of worship*. Instead, the meaning of the word *cult* can now be said to lie in the eyes of the beholder. Rather than protest the change, we must acknowledge the ever-changing nature of the English language and work with what we have inherited. We must recognize the new use of the word as it is commonly used in the world of religion—especially in the pejorative sense. But even within the narrowed focus of religion, the term has multiple meanings. It is used to describe groups ranging from societies of dangerous fanaticism on the one extreme, to those who simply hold one or more "unorthodox" theological views on the other.

Therefore, in my attempt to answer the question raised by the title of this book, I started by surveying what others have identified as being the defining marks of a religious cult. The result of this investigation was a collection of 23 social-structural, social-psychological, and interpersonal behavioral patterns commonly used to identify what is deemed "cultic" behavior. These traits are what others say about today's religious cults—characteristics that are now commonly used by modern society

---

1. "The Scent of a Cult," *First Things*, January 1995.

to identify a religious cult. With this list at hand, we will compare each characteristic with its applicability to the Christadelphians—a relatively small Christian fellowship that can be traced back to the early 19th century Restoration Movement.[2]

Cult Characteristic # 1 — A Charismatic Leader

One of the most common characteristics of a Christian cult is the presence of an authoritarian leader over whom there is no meaningful accountability. The group's leader is viewed as always right, he/she is the exclusive means of knowing "truth" or receiving validation, and no other process of discovery is acceptable or credible. A cult displays excessively zealous and unquestioning commitment to its leader (whether dead or alive) and regards its belief system, ideology, and practices as the absolute truth—as law. The leader is always right, and their misdeeds are always justified. Criticism of the leader is forbidden. The leader of a cult may be seen as *a* or *the* "Messiah," a special being, an avatar (incarnation), or viewed as a person on a special mission to save humanity. The leader is not accountable to any authorities unlike, for example, teachers, military commanders, ministers, priests, monks, or rabbis of mainstream religious denominations.

This attribute, however, does not apply to the Christadelphians. At no time during their century and a half existence have they ever had such a figurehead in place. Instead, Jesus is regarded as the Head of each congregation (which they call *ecclesias* instead of *churches*). Christadelphians do not have paid ministers. Functions within Christadelphian

---

2. The Restoration Movement began in the United States and was a reform effort within Christianity which resulted in the development of non-denominational churches which stressed reliance on scripture and few essentials. It is also commonly referred to as the "Stone-Campbell Movement." Today, the three main groups that have some historical ties with this movement are known as the "Churches of Christ," the "Disciples of Christ," and the "Christian Church." The original movement sought Christian reform based upon the Bible alone as a sufficient guide and rejected all creeds. However, this liberality eventually led to dissent which then led to the formation of the Christadelphians in the 1860s. Opposition to this movement's doctrinal liberality was led by an English medical doctor named John Thomas, who played an important role in the development and naming of the Christadelphians. A more detailed history of the Restoration Movement and the formation of the Christadelphians is provided in Chapters 8 and 9.

communities are operated by volunteers. Male members are assessed over time by the congregation for their eligibility to teach and perform various duties, which are usually assigned on a rotational basis, as opposed to having a permanently appointed preacher. This congregational governance typically follows a democratic model resulting in each ecclesia being run by an unpaid group of "elders" who are responsible for the day-to-day affairs of the body and who are answerable to the rest of the ecclesia's members.

Those who are elected to the position of elder serve for a limited time, and while they are in office, are responsible for "overseeing the flock." This is viewed as an honor, and it is used as an opportunity to serve others. Such an autonomous arrangement, which has been in place for more than a century, makes it difficult for a single authoritarian figure to arise and to influence the worldwide community. Although some members over time get higher status as exceptional speakers or wield more influence in their individual ecclesias on account of their age, their knowledge, wisdom, experience, or due to family ties, such members rarely abuse their position. In a worst case scenario, should it ever occur, abuse of power is confined to that single congregation alone.

Christadelphians respect, admire and are grateful to the individuals who played an important role in the formation and growth of their movement, but they do not view such individuals as faultless. In other words, the 19th century "pioneers" of the Christadelphian movement are not considered sacrosanct, and are subject to criticism as well as praise.

Cult Characteristic # 2 — Central Organization

The Catholic Church has Rome, the Jehovah's Witnesses have their Watchtower Society in Brooklyn, New York, and the Mormons have Salt Lake City, Utah. In contrast, Christadelphians are decentralized and congregations do not answer to any central organization or headquarters. They claim to be guided by the Bible, not by any "mother church" or worldwide committee.

One striking feature of the Christadelphians is their non-hierarchical organization. Each ecclesia is responsible for its own affairs. They all accept a common basis of belief, but its implementation is left to each individual ecclesia. Each congregation is entirely independent and autonomous from the other, yet they all remain in the wider fellowship through a shared group of doctrines. The independence of each ecclesia has always been guarded and the rights of conscience and private judgment have always remained recognized. Such ecclesial independence is another reason why any hostile report from a disgruntled former member should not be viewed as characteristic of the body worldwide.

As noted previously, within each ecclesia, service is undertaken by members appointed for limited periods who are answerable to the whole congregation. The administration of each congregation is undertaken by the completely voluntary assistance of lay members.

Cult Characteristic # 3 — Distancing Oneself from Society

Inducing a loss of reality by physical separation from family, friends, and society is another characteristic of what is commonly viewed as belonging to a cult. This goes beyond cutting off contact with non-member friends and family members. Cults encourage or require members to live and/or socialize only with other group members in order to promote total dependence on the group or its leader(s). Unless they are actively engaged in trying to convert a non-member to the group, a member's contact with outsiders is extremely minimal. This could simply mean that they don't engage with outsiders in their everyday lives (e.g., talking to others is disallowed), or it could be as drastic as choosing to live among members and refusing to acknowledge that there is an outside world at all.

Christadelphians, in contrast, maintain social connections with those outside of their faith community. Christadelphians maintain normal relationships with non-Christadelphians just as long as that relationship does not discredit their Christian witness, cause them to take their eyes off the kingdom of God, or cause weak members among them to stumble.

Christadelphians are self-motivated in keeping up-to-date with world events, particularly as they relate to Bible prophecy and Jesus' return to the earth. Christadelphians are exposed daily to the outside world with all of the tragic news accompanying it, yet they do not seek for an escape by isolating themselves into communes or withdrawing from society, traits often found within a cult.

Cult Characteristic # 4 — Peer Group Pressure

Group pressure is another sign of a cult, such as when a person is carefully managed, constantly monitored, and manipulated through subtle forms of peer persuasion. This may include the threat or use of punishment (material, social, and emotional) through the normative rules of the community, or through peer monitoring which seeks for any expressions of reservations or dissent. If these things are present in a group, there is the potential that it is a cult.

In contrast, Christadelphians believe people must live and act according to convictions they form from reading their Bibles and not from trends from outside or pressure from within. Whether it be matters of externals (clothing, fashion, education, entertainment, career), or matters of internals (doctrinal beliefs or opinions), Christadelphians attempt to seek first what the Scriptures say rather than what man says. Christadelphians are encouraged to think for themselves, to question and debate issues and to make reasoned decisions.

Having said that, this is not to say that Christadelphians do not hold each other accountable when a member goes astray, leaving the straight and narrow way that Jesus tells his disciples they must walk. Ecclesial discipline, though rarely used, is a Biblical injunction whenever a brother or sister in Christ openly lives in sin and refuses to repent after multiple attempts to speak sensibly and lovingly to them and in accordance with Matthew 18:15-17. Among Christadelphians, such disciplinary actions are a last resort.

Cult Characteristic # 5 — Loss of Independence

In a cult, the leader or a group of leaders dictates—sometimes in great detail—how members should think, act, and feel. For example, members must get permission to date, change jobs, marry, or leaders prescribe what type of clothes to wear, where to live, whether or not to have children, how to discipline children, and so forth.

In contrast, Christadelphians exercise a great deal of independence and do not have rules placed upon them pertaining to such matters as family size, housing location, child raising, finances/spending, diet or special dress code (although in some regions some women practice covering their hair during worship services).

It is a Christadelphian goal to "marry only in the Lord," as the apostle Paul admonished in 1 Corinthians 7:39, but such a position is nothing out of the norm for any religious group who takes their identity seriously, be they Jewish, Catholic, or any stripe of Bible-believing Christian.

When it comes to occupations, no rules are laid upon a Christadelphian other than whatever path they have chosen to earn a living should not dishonor Jesus or place them in a position of compromising their faith or witness—again, common-sense guidelines that any serious disciple of Jesus—no matter what denomination they belong to—would endorse.

Cult Characteristic # 6 — Manipulating Emotions

Cults often manipulate a convert's emotions through group-ecstatic practices, including repetitious chanting, hand clapping, dancing, laughing fits, shouting, highly charged musical performances, flag waving, outbursts, mystical insights, private revelations, and miracle cures—all of which incite emotional responses rather than encourage rational conclusions. Christadelphian services do not use any such methods of disinhibition or emotional pleas.

Within a Christadelphian meeting, emotion arises only from an individual's contemplation of the scripture message and not from any applied "techniques" to stimulate it. Christadelphian meetings and services do not rely on artificial means to impress teachings upon the listeners. Generally speaking, meetings consist of hymns, Bible readings, prayers and Bible-based talks. They are always calm, ordered and devotional. For anyone who is used to "worship pomp"—the pageantry of high ecclesiasticalism, the hand waving energy produced by guitars and drums at the heart of contemporary music, large choirs, and charismatic preachers who entertain while they preach—such individuals will find Christadelphian meetings downright boring in comparison.

Cult Characteristic # 7 — Love-Bombing

Cults often start seducing people with love-bombing, that is, paying a great deal of attention to and being very affectionate with potential recruits. It can be a very effective way of connecting with someone who is feeling lonely and isolated. The process creates a sense of family and belonging through hugging, kissing, touching and flattery. New people are invited to dinner, quizzed intensely about their past, offered home-cooked meals and support around the home, and eventually have their calendar filled with social events with existing cult members. All of the niceness prompts initiates to let their barriers down. The result is that appropriate boundaries aren't in place when the new members are eventually made to do things that would have once felt uncomfortable doing.

Since each Christadelphian ecclesia is an independent entity, it would be unwise to make universal statements about how visitors are treated when they first make contact with a Christadelphian. Obviously, there is nothing wrong with any host (in this case the ecclesia) rolling out the red carpet when a guest graces their meeting place, and since most ecclesias tend to be small in number, any visitor is bound to draw attention. It is not uncommon for visitors to Sunday morning services to later be invited to lunch, where of course, the individuals can better get to know each other, assuming the guest is interested. This is nothing more than what the New Testament expects of Christians, for they are instructed, "Don't neglect to show hospitality, for by doing this some have welcomed angels as guests without knowing it" (Hebrews 13:2). There is a clear difference between the love-bombing practiced by a cult, and simple, down-home hospitality shown to a new person visiting a Christadelphian ecclesia.

When I first had the opportunity to set foot in a Christadelphian meeting-place, unquestionably I drew attention. In a congregation that consisted of 3-4 dozen individuals, it is hard to hide. But in that visit, and subsequent visits, I was never hugged, kissed, or flattered. Nor was it a surprise that southern hospitality and basic Christian charity resulted in an invitation to lunch after the worship service was over, suggested by one married couple. But once that meal was over, there was no further contact made with any Christadelphian until I decided on my own volition to pay them a second visit. I believe that my experience was not atypical. You may call it what you'd like—an example of being nice or simply showing hospitality—in either case, it surely wasn't cultic love-bombing.

Cult Characteristic # 8 — Time Manipulation

Time control is used by cults to keep their members so busy with meetings and activities that they become immersed in the manufactured cult environment to the point of having no free time. Members of a cult are expected to devote inordinate amounts of time to the group—this can include completing jobs or performing missions for the group or participating in other group-related activities. Friends and family members of cult members—assuming ties to them haven't already been cut off—will notice and often comment on the fact that they never seem to see their loved one anymore.

Christadelphians, on the other hand, spend just as much time with family, in leisure activities, in sleep and pursuing education and career as the average member of society. Despite their busyness in the cares of normal life, they, like all Christians, are reminded by the Bible to "number our days, that we may apply our hearts unto wisdom" (Psalms 90:12). This means that their aim is to avoid wasting time in frivolous and harmful pursuits that run contrary to the admonition to "Redeem the time, because the days are evil" (Ephesians 5:16). Some are more successful than others at this goal. Worldly ambitions, daily distractions and time-wasting pursuits abound. However, the bottom line is that Christadelphians are not beholden to serve any organization or earthly leader, nor are they required to be at every ecclesial event or forced to perform any mandated activities. Instead, they are instructed to voluntarily love and serve God with all their heart and their neighbor as themselves in whatever forms opportunity and time may allow.

Cult Characteristic # 9 — Mind-altering Practices

Indoctrination or "brainwashing" is the process through which a cult slowly breaks down a person's sense of identity and ability to think rationally. Such a state is often achieved through mind altering practices which are done repeatedly. Mind control is any totalistic system of influence that disrupts an individual's authentic identity and replaces it with a false, new one. Behaviors like excessive fasting/starvation, mandatory and formulaic prayers, hypnosis, or drug usage can all be used to increase a person's vulnerability to the cult leader's suggestions.

Mind control techniques may include Transcendental Meditation and the use of mantras, chanting, speaking in tongues, denunciation sessions, debilitating work routines, or the taking of psychotropic drugs or psychedelic substances. The goal is to alter the emotional state of members, and to blur their perception of reality, subjecting them to systematic behavior, information, thoughts, and emotions to keep them dependent and obedient.

Christadelphians do not alter their minds through the use of any of these methods. The only "mind-altering" practices that Christadelphians encourage are the reading, reflection, and studying of the Old and New Testaments, along with personal prayer in keeping with the admonition to "be transformed by the renewing of your mind, so that you may discern what is the good, pleasing, and perfect will of God" (Romans 12:2, CSB).

Cult Characteristic # 10 — Coercion to Convert

Fear and guilt are central to any thought reform/mind control program. A fearful person is one who cannot think critically and whose ability to make decisions is reduced. Cult tactics include inducing fears and phobias (strong, irrational fears) in group members to allow the leadership to maintain control. Members can believe that all sorts of horrible things may happen if they don't follow the rules. Even the most devoted members fear what may happen to them should they choose to leave (or even consider leaving) the group.

Pressuring or scaring would-be members into conversion is absent from Christadelphian communities. And although parents attempt to raise their children "in the nurture and admonition of the Lord" (Ephesians 6:4), Christadelphian children are free to reject their parent's faith if they so wish.[3] With more and more frequency they appear to be doing just that, with most children choosing to follow the way of the world and not make any Christian commitment whatsoever.

Within the Christadelphian community, no one is asked to commit him or herself to Jesus quickly. Everyone is given ample time to consider carefully the implications of accepting God's gracious offer of salvation, and of the responsibilities of discipleship. This is especially important since the Christadelphians can readily be classified as a "high commitment group," due to their non-conformist stance on many matters, both in doctrine and practice, which requires a steadfast willingness to carry one's cross and not be conformed to the world around them (cf. Matthew 16:24, Romans 12:2).

Christadelphians do not specially target any particular group in society. They do not approach only young people or children; they do not focus specially upon women and not on men. Any special activities for children, such as Sunday Schools, are completely open to the parents as well, and their content consists of basic Bible instruction.

Cult Characteristic # 11 — Leaving the Cult (Breaking Up is Hard to Do)

Another characteristic of modern cults is their unreasonable control of individual members. Frequently, great emotional pressure is applied to any person who wishes to leave the group. If this pressure is resisted and all formal ties with the group are cut, the individual is completely shunned and treated as an outcast. All social contact is ended and the person is considered as good as dead.

In contrast, if an individual wishes to leave the Christadelphian community, they are free to do so. The one who has left will not be badgered or hounded to return. Naturally, other members will wish to discuss the decision to leave with them, but they will not force their presence on the one who wishes to depart, or coerce the dissenter to refrain from leaving, but rather will respect their ultimate decision. If the one who desires to leave has been with the community for a long time, it may be disorienting to find close friends within the community suddenly become distant, avoiding the close fellowship that previously

---

3. Although the children of devout Christadelphians will feel some unspoken pressure from their parents on account of not wanting to disappoint them, this situation is no different than in any religion, be it Christian, Muslim or Jewish.

existed. But it would only be fair to look at this from the other side, too. In the eyes of the Christadelphians, the one who has departed is seen as having rejected the community, not the other way around. Anyone who has been in a romantic relationship and been dumped by their partner knows what this feels like. It is only to be expected that hurt feelings will exist between the parties, even if the breakup was civil and drama-free.

Cult Characteristic # 12 — Preoccupied with Bringing in New Members

There's one thing that a cult likes more than its own members: adding new members. Bringing more people "into the fold" is a definite ego boost to the cult leader, who feels powerful for having control over a growing number of people. Additionally, new members usually means more money flowing into the coffers (see characteristic #13).

Perhaps somewhat to their own regret and shame, Christadelphians put minimal effort into the evangelization of others here in the English-speaking West. They do, however, send missionaries (supported by voluntary donations) to the non-Western world. But here in the West, they rarely practice door-to-door canvassing, nor the distribution of tracts, and are less and less found participating in public preaching events.

In all fairness, much of this non-engagement is not due to a lack of desire or a failure to appreciate the importance of evangelization. Rather it can be traced to the overall societal decline in interest in the Bible which results in few new prospects. In predominantly English-speaking countries, Christadelphians instead focus their energies on building up their ecclesial family rather than on evangelism. Any outreach to outsiders is typically done at a personal, individual level, among family, friends, and coworkers, through the building of relationships and sharing of Scripture, and is not part of institutional-wide or mandated campaigns.

Cult Characteristic # 13 — Preoccupied with Asking for Money

Cults can't survive on good feelings alone. They need money. There is often a business front to a cult, whether they are selling a product, service, or their lifestyle brand. Cult leaders often lavish themselves with luxuries, such as Rolls Royces and private jets while members are instructed to collect money in less than honest ways. Promises that prosperity and divine blessings will ensue, including miracles, are commonly made. And as one might expect, never is there enough money, which leads to members being encouraged to give their offerings even if it means putting their families in financial risk.

Since Christadelphians have no central organization, headquarters, or paid clergy or administrative staff to sustain, the focus on raising money is absent among the community. It helps that a significant number of Christadelphian ecclesias do not own their places of worship, but rather rent modest community centers or halls, which reduces the need for donations. Among those few which do own their own buildings, the structures will all be found to have no distinctive architectural features and will be modest, plain, and void of ornateness.

Many Christadelphian ecclesias eschew the common "passing of the offering plate" in exchange for a simple, out-of-the-way collection box or bag where offerings can be made without pressure or fanfare. Christadelphians do not teach that there is any obligation to tithe or give a percentage of one's income. Individuals contribute financially as they see fit, not according to rules or requirements imposed upon them. What members contribute is regarded as a personal matter. Pyramid schemes, get rich quick seminars, multi-level-marketing scams, and lavish building proposals are unheard of in their community.

Cult Characteristic # 14 — Hidden Finances

If you're not allowed to know what the group does with its money, then perhaps you're in a cult, for cults frequently hide their financial records from their members. In a cult, no meaningful financial disclosure exists regarding budgets or expenses, such as an independently audited financial statement.

In contrast, any Christadelphian ecclesia that consists of more than just a handful of family members, and who have a system of collecting gifts and offerings, will have a treasurer who will report its finances at a regular business meeting to which all its members are welcome to attend and review the financial information provided.

Cult Characteristic # 15 — Communal Living and Forfeiture of Private Property

Extremist cults are often—in varying degrees—communal in nature, withdrawing from the world and isolating themselves in private tight-knit communities. Such societies swear off private property and have all worldly possessions in common. Christadelphians, although willing to share with others, do not live communally, but maintain private property, owning their own homes and independently renting their own apartments. There are no Christadelphian monasteries, communal houses, or privately run societies or communities.

Cult Characteristic # 16 — The End Justifies the Means

Modern cults often teach or imply that their supposedly exalted ends justify whatever means it deems necessary to achieve them. This may result in members participating in behaviors or activities they would have considered reprehensible, unlawful or unethical before joining the group (for example, lying to family or friends, or collecting money for bogus charities).

In contrast, Christadelphians are in agreement with the apostle Paul's response expressed in Romans 3:6, "shall we sin, because we are not under the law, but under grace? God forbid." Paul likewise reported that it was a slander disseminated by his enemies that he was teaching "Let us do evil, that good may come" (v. 8). Christadelphians take Paul's words here so much to heart that they abstain even from politics and military combat.

Cult Characteristic # 17 — Unique Practices and Taboos

The term *cult* has become synonymous with socially deviant and/ or unique practices or rituals. When examining Christianity, we can find unique practices among the Roman Catholics, who have celibate priests, rosaries, and confessionals, to name a few. Within the Jehovah's Witnesses, there is a ban on blood transfusions and birthday celebrations. Along with the Jehovah's Witnesses, the Worldwide Church of God (of Herbert W. Armstrong) bans celebrating Christmas and Easter. Among Mormons, baptisms are performed for dead people and the consumption of alcohol and "hot drinks" is prohibited.[4] Christadelphians, on the other hand, hold to no unique practice associated with their faith. They have no particular diets, or secret oaths or handshakes or hand gestures, no mystical utterances or codewords, no special undergarments, no religious vestments, and no objects of veneration. Nor do they prohibit dancing, the consumption of alcohol, cosmetics for women, ear piercing, tattoos, facial hair, or the use of modern medicine (including psychiatry). Holidays such as Easter, Halloween and Christmas are not banned, although many choose not to observe them. They do not proscribe hair length, choice of clothing, musical preferences, or entertainment choices. Christadelphians follow the words of Colossians 2:16 that the disciples of Jesus are not to judge in terms of meat, drink, holy days, new moons, or sabbaths.

Cult Characteristic # 18 — Distortion of Human Sexuality

One of the hallmarks of a cult is the corruption and distortion of human sexuality. This is manifested either in excess or in deprivation. In contrast, Christadelphians have always taught against premarital sex, adultery, polygamy, homosexuality, and bisexuality, and other forms of sexual immorality. Nor do Christadelphians advocate celibacy or singleness above marriage, for as Hebrews 13:4 states, "Marriage is to be honored by all and the marriage bed kept undefiled."

---

4. Mormons are permitted to drink herbal teas and hot chocolate milk. Drinks made from coffee beans and tea trees, however, are banned.

Cult Characteristic # 19 — Hiding the Truth, Hiding the Past

Information is power. But once inside a cult, information is controlled. Once you're among the ranks of a cult, the organization will slam the door on questioning. Destructive cults often conceal or misrepresent information that would have resulted in many different choices in the lives of their members had the truth been known. In other words, had members been fully informed about the cult prior to joining, they would not have joined. Or, had those who were born into the cult been fully informed during their coming of age, they would have left at the earliest opportunity. Then there are others, who had the means to access information and discover the truth about the cult all along, but were instead guided by emotion and fear. Rather than seeking and finding information, critically examining it, and making informed decisions, they avoided initiating their own escape.

It could be said that Christadelphians as a whole are a very skeptical bunch, taking as their motto, "Examine all things; hold fast to what is good" (1 Thessalonians 5:2). Perhaps their next favorite verse when it comes to examining matters of faith comes from Acts 17:11, "These [the Bereans] were more noble than those in Thessalonica, in that they received the word with all readiness of mind, and searched the scriptures daily, whether those things were so." This is one way of saying that Christadelphians regularly practice self-examination, both individually and collectively. They do this in their periodicals, and in the Internet age, through on-line discussion groups, questionnaires, and forums. They invite investigation and don't shy away from examining their past. They make it easy to obtain archival material, and regularly reprint articles, pamphlets, and books written by their pioneers more than a century ago, making it possible for anyone to critically examine and compare their teachings and words as time passed.

For more nearly forty years, this author has sought for a skeleton in the Christadelphian closet. From that first day when I entered the U.S. Library of Congress with the words *Christadelphians* and *cult* both on my lips, seeking for dusty writings from their early years, I have been unable to find such a skeleton, despite having combed hundreds of volumes of their books and periodicals. The most I can point to is an occasional Christadelphian writer who took a stab at trying to interpret Bible prophecy and went out on a limb to identify the year of Jesus' return, and got it wrong. See the next "characteristic" for more on this topic.

Cult Characteristic # 20 — Paranoia, Bunker Mentality, and Date Setting

When criticized or attacked by outsiders, a cult quickly responds defensively, believing that they are being wrongly attacked or criticized by others rather than examining whether there be any truth in the criticisms. Blaming outside enemies is used as an excuse to avoid self-examination and correction. Repeated attacks lead to unreasonable fear and catastrophic thinking about the outside world. Evil conspiracy theories are then posited by the group and the outsiders' actions are labeled as persecutions. Often the fears extend to a belief of impending catastrophe.

With respect to impending catastrophes, the Christadelphians believe Jesus' return will be accompanied with signs as described in the Olivet Prophecy: "And great earthquakes shall be in divers places, and famines, and pestilences; and fearful sights and great signs shall there be from heaven....there shall be signs in the sun, and in the moon, and in the stars; and upon the earth distress of nations, with perplexity; the sea and the waves roaring..." (Luke 21:11,25). Though believing that Jesus' return is imminent, modern Christadelphians do not make pronouncements on "the day or the hour" of his return (Matthew 24:36). It is true that as enthusiastic Bible students, some prominent Christadelphians within their denomination's 150-year history have attempted to decipher the prophetic calendars described in the books of Daniel and Revelation and cautiously forecasted a year. Attempts have been made by some within their ranks to understand the meaning of the prophet Daniel's seventy weeks (Daniel 9:24), the 1290 days (Daniel 12:11), the 1335 days (Daniel 12:12) and 2300 days (Daniel 8:14), including Revelation's 1260 days (Revelation 11:3, 12:6). But these attempts by scattered individuals to provide commentary on the prophetic calendar have never turned into dogmatic pronouncements embraced by the collective community on the "day and the hour" of Jesus' return. Christadelphians are too ecclesiastically independent and too skeptical of self-proclaimed revelators to fall in lockstep with private interpretations of the prophetic calendar, or to sell all their possessions and gather on some mountain-top awaiting Jesus' descent. Nor have they ever stockpiled weapons and foodstuffs to carry them through some upcoming apocalypse.

Due to their fiercely independent and ecclesiastically autonomous makeup, they fare exceptionally better than some other religious bodies and individuals who have made themselves a laughing-stock more than once through their over-confident date assertions. A failure to recognize that an individual within an independently autonomous community providing a chronology or commentary on the prophetic calendar does not speak on behalf of the entire community is one of the frequent failures of critics of the Christadelphians. For example, a critic will search hard to discover and then cite a Christadelphian commentator from the 19th-century who independently believed that the end of Daniel's 2300 days was to be accomplished in 1860's and then pass judgment on the entire Christadelphian community over the past 150 years because that single commentator was wrong. Critics who use such tactics need to bear in mind the vital difference between understanding Bible teaching concerning doctrine (first principles) and interpreting prophecy. Failing to make this distinction would be equivalent to condemning Isaac Newton's laws of motion and universal gravitation on account of Newton, as a theologian, determining that the year 2016 would mark the end of the 1260 "day for a year" period described in the book of Revelation. Yes, Newton in fact made such a calculation.[5]

In fact, such attempts to discern "the times and seasons" are nothing new to Christianity. Newton was only agreeing with what many Protestant theologians and Bible commentators of his day were saying. The best Protestant Bible interpreters at that time, which included Jonathan Edwards, Robert Fleming, Moses Lowman, Phillip Doddridge, and Bishop Thomas Newton, were pretty well agreed that the 1260-year time-line found in the book of Revelation would end in 2016.[6] Should we therefore condemn all of the Protestant denominations associated with these 18th-century theologians (such as the Church of England, the Puritans, Presbyterians, Congregationalists and the Reformed Churches) and label them as "cults" just because a few of their members attempted to discern prophetic dates and numbers and got it wrong?

---

5. Newton later adjusted his calculation to the year 2060. See https://en.wikipedia.org/wiki/Religious_views_of_Isaac_Newton#2016_vs._2060 (accessed Aug. 30, 2022).

And yet the Christadelphians are sometimes unfairly criticized, condemned, and classified as a cult once it is discovered that a small handful of their Bible commentators were just as unsuccessful at date-setting as some of the brightest theologians of the 18th-century.

Cult Characteristic # 21 — Unique Scripture

Many cults have their own unique writings which they either substitute for the Bible or add to the Bible. In contrast, Christadelphians do not treat any extra-Biblical books or writings as Holy Scripture. Unlike the Roman Catholic Church which includes apocryphal books such as *3 Maccabees* and *Bel and the Dragon* as part of their inspired Bible, and unlike the Mormons who add the *Book of Mormon, Doctrine and Covenants,* and the *Pearl of Great Price* and place them on equal footing with the Bible, Christadelphians embrace the same 66 books of the Bible as do mainstream Protestants and add nothing more to the collection of inspired writings that they follow.

Among some conservative, old-school Christadelphian ecclesias, the writings of two men in particular—John Thomas and Robert Roberts (see chapters 8 & 9)—are held in high esteem on account of the role they played in the formation and development of the Christadelphian faith. Their writings are not elevated to the level of holy writ, but are rather used as benchmarks to compare whether modern Christadelphians have perhaps drifted from their roots over time. This deference is similar to Lutherans referring to the views of Martin Luther, or the Reformed faith interacting with the works of John Calvin.

---

6. Jonathan Edwards, *History of Redemption* (New York: T. and J. Swords, 1793), p. 431: "*The* BEGINNING *of the reign of Antichrist.*] The best interpreters (as Mr. Fleming, Sir I. Newton, Mr. Lowman, Dr. Doddridge, Bp. Newton, and Mr. Reader) are pretty well agreed that this reign is to be dated from about A.D. 756, when the Pope began to be a temporal power, (that is, in prophetic language, a *beast*) by assuming temporal dominion; 1260 years from this period will bring us to about A. D. 2000, and about the 6000th year of the world, which agrees with a tradition at least as ancient as the epistle ascribed to the apostle Barnabas [§ 15.] which says, that "in six thousand years shall all things be accomplished."

Cult Characteristic # 22 — Unique Translation/Version of the Bible

The Roman Catholic Church and the Jehovah's Witnesses have their own, uniquely approved translations of the Bible that they rely upon and stress that their members use at the exclusion of others. Christadelphians, in contrast, have no favorite Bible translation and encourage the use of multiple translations in order to consider alternative points of view when it comes to understanding a Bible passage. Christadelphians do not rely on any particular translation of the Bible to support their beliefs.

Cult Characteristic # 23 — Unique, Novel Doctrines, and Revelations

Emphasizing special doctrines or practices that are outside of the Bible is another trait of today's cult. Doctrines such as the belief in Purgatory, or that Jesus' mother Mary was miraculously born and never died but was taken directly up into heaven, or the belief that the Kingdom of God will be centered in Salt Lake City, Utah, or that the Native American Indians are one of the lost tribes of Israel, or that blood transfusions are banned by the Bible—all of these novel doctrines are found among other "Christian" religious groups. According to those who study cults, extra-Biblical doctrines (that is, teachings that originate outside of the pages of the Bible) are common in cults.

Christadelphians, however, do not hold to any doctrine that is unique to them. In other words, each of the doctrines that mark Christadelphians as being out of the mainstream of Christianity can be found taught within either another well-established Christian denomination or within first century Judaism. The doctrines embraced by the Christadelphians consist of only those that were taught, practiced, or believed in the first ten years of the first century Church.

Cults often claim they've been given a "special revelation" from God that is superior to the Bible. The cult leader or group claims a supernatural communication from God that has been given only to him or them. Christadelphians have never advocated for any new doctrine beyond what could already be found within the first century Church.

They also make no claim to special knowledge beyond what a diligent reader can obtain from a careful reading of the Bible.

Why Then the Cult Label?

If none of the above twenty-plus "cultic" behaviors[7] apply to the Christadelphians, why then can you go on the Internet, type a web search for "Christadelphians" and find numerous pages describing the Christadelphians as a cult? I will address this question in the next two chapters.

---

7. I want to make it clear that this list of cult behaviors was a compilation of what other writers have put forward. I did not create or devise any of the previously listed behaviors, but rather wanted to see what society currently identifies as characteristics of a cult, and then compare those definitions against Christadelphian practice.

CHAPTER 3

An Online Example

The biggest problem is that Facebook and Google are these giant feedback loops that give people what they want to hear. And when you use them in a world where your biases are being constantly confirmed, you become susceptible to fake news, propaganda, demagoguery.[1]

—FRANKLIN FOER

WHEN I BEGAN this writing project I had no intention of turning it into a book. Instead, my intention was to present a single lecture on this topic, and after that, to move on to other things. In the process of preparing that lecture, I decided to share how the Christadelphians are often portrayed by others outside of their community and that the greatest source of negative publicity comes from the Internet. At that time, an online search for the phrase "Are Christadelphians a cult?" using the search engine Google, generated among its highest ranking search results an item titled, "Is Christadelphianism Christian?" Linked to that item was an article written by Matt Slick, who belongs to an organization called Christian Apologetics & Research Ministry (CARM). Today, his article no longer bubbles up to the top of the search results, but it did in 2020.

His article purportedly examined "Christadelphianism," but what it actually did was illustrate how frequently and to what extent those who I call "heresy hunters" misrepresent the Christadelphians. Slick's article began rather succinctly:

No, Christadelphianism is not Christian.[2]

---

1. Tom McCarthy, "Franklin Foer: 'Big tech has been rattled. The conversation has changed,'" *The Guardian*, October 19, 2017, https://theguardian.com/technology/2017/oct/19/big-tech-franklin-foer-book-world-without-mind (accessed September 3, 2022).

What followed next, consisting of roughly 1000 words, was his explanation why Christadelphians are not Christian. To characterize these 1000 words as "research" seems like a stretch, especially when several of the available paragraphs mislead the reader, such as the following:

> Like all cults, Christadelphianism denies one or more of the essential doctrines of Christianity: Jesus is God, the physical resurrection, and salvation by grace. In this case, it is the deity of Christ and salvation by grace through faith that are the problems with this group.[3]

It should be quickly pointed out that the Christadelphians unequivocally believe that Jesus died and rose back to life three days after his death with a physical body. There has never been any question at any time about this truth within the Christadelphian community.

As to the other two traits of a Christian cult identified by Slick, I will begin with the last item first (i.e., salvation by grace through faith), for it doesn't take much "research" or time to demonstrate how this is a false accusation against the Christadelphians. Later in this chapter, I will address the matter of "the deity of Christ."

Salvation By Grace

Contrary to Slick's claim, Christadelphians do in fact believe that salvation is by the grace of God, through faith. Christadelphians readily confess that they cannot earn their salvation, as the following examples (taken fairly recently from one of their leading international periodicals) confirm.

---

2. Matt Slick, "Are Christadelphians a cult?," *Christian Apologetics & Research Ministry*, https://carm.org/is-christadelphianism-christian (accessed March 19, 2019).

3. Ibid. With respect to "the physical resurrection," while Slick did not level a charge against the Christadelphians on this point, it is worth pointing out that Slick does not distinguish whether this is a reference to the resurrection of Jesus, or to the resurrection of the "dead in Christ," or both. Either way, Christadelphians unquestionably believe that Jesus rose back to life three days after his death with a physical body. They also believe that those who are dead and asleep "in Christ" will likewise rise from the dead when Jesus returns to the earth to establish his Father's kingdom.

John's letters link faith and love, as if to show that the two are inextricably bound together. Having real faith means that we are not "slothful" (Hebrews 6:12); the cloying laziness of our natures will be brushed aside by the imperative to action which faith gives. And "in the truth", the propositions of "the one faith", we have the motivating power which no other religion or sect of Christendom can offer. Time and again, faith and works are bracketed together. Abraham was justified by faith, Paul argues in Romans; and by works, says James. Even within Genesis, his faith was counted for righteousness in Genesis 15; but Genesis 22:15–18 stress that because he had "*done* this thing" and been obedient, thereby he was justified. [...]

There is a beauty to all this, in that salvation is by faith that it might be by grace (Romans 4:16; Ephesians 2:8). In this sense, salvation is not by works. But if we can comprehend something of the purity of that grace, of God's willingness to save us regardless of our works; then we will *believe* it. And *if* we believe it, we will live a life of active working for the Lord—not that we might be saved, but in thankful faith and gratitude for the magnitude of our experience of a grace, the height and depth of which, unfathomed, no man knows.

—Duncan Heaster, "Faith in God," *The Christadelphian*, vol. 136, no. 1626, December 1999, p. 446.

How thankful we should be that, although we have a part to play in forsaking our wickedness and expressing faith through baptism, our salvation does not depend upon ourselves or any human agency.

—John S. Roberts, "Spent in Vain," *The Christadelphian*, vol. 140, March 2003, p. 81.

We learn from Scripture and from our experiences in life, that we have no righteousness of our own. There is no covering that we can manufacture that will hide our guilt. Paul writes,

"For by grace are ye saved through faith; and that not of yourselves: it is the gift of God: not of works, lest any man should
boast. For we are his workmanship, created in Christ Jesus
unto good works, which God hath before ordained that we
should walk in them" (Ephesians 2:8-10).

There can be no human boasting in our salvation, only a deep
thankfulness that God's covering never fails for those who
truly trust Him. The good works we do, and must do, are
therefore to the glory of God and not ourselves.

> —Malcolm Edwards, "The Lesson of Leaves and Fruit," *The
> Christadelphian*, vol. 139, no. 1652, February 2002, p. 42.

Yet, with the benefit of the New Testament, and particularly
the letter to the Hebrews, we can look beyond what might otherwise seem tedious detail and see in it "the patterns of things
in the heavens"; we gain precious insights into the divine mind
and into the wonder of our salvation by grace through Jesus
Christ our Lord.

> — Geoff Henstock, "God Dwelling with Men," *The Christadel-
> phian*, vol. 147, no. 1751, May 2010, p. 174.

These quotes were gleaned from just one Christadelphian periodical within roughly a 10-year time span. Additional quotes contradicting
the "research" of CARM on this one point could easily be provided from
additional Christadelphian periodicals and books spanning more than
one hundred years. Of course these quotes do not fully explain the
Christadelphian view on salvation, therefore let us now continue our
examination of their views to see how CARM repeatedly misrepresents
the Christadelphian position.

Christadelphians acknowledge that salvation is by grace, through
faith in Jesus the Messiah. At the same time they are mindful that Paul
instructs the Philippians to "work out your own salvation with fear and
trembling" (Philippians 2:12)—an admonition to Christians that they
are called to follow and walk after the *example* and *teachings* of Jesus.
Among such examples and teachings left by Jesus to his followers is the

rite of baptism. And it is their obedient attitude towards this rite that Matt Slick uses as evidence that the terms "cult" and "non-Christian" should be applied to the Christadelphians. Partly on account of their belief that baptism is a commandment which Christians are to obey rather than something which can be treated as an option, Slick charges that Christadelphians do not believe in "salvation by grace," stating:

> ... the Christadelphians add a work to salvation. They say that baptism is part of the saving process. But, baptism is not necessary for salvation. Instead, it is a representation of the inward reality of regeneration (1 Pet. 3:21), a covenant sign of God's work upon the heart (Col. 2:11-12). Additionally, Rom. 5:1 says that we are justified by faith, not by faith and baptism. Rom. 3:28 says we are saved not by the works of the Law; that is, not by anything that we do.[4]

One would expect a knowledgeable "Bible researcher" to know that baptism is not a "work of the Law" but rather it is a teaching and commandment of Jesus. As part of the Great Commission, Jesus instructed his disciples:

> Go ye therefore, and teach all nations, baptizing them...
> (Matthew 28:19, KJV)

Furthermore, underscoring the need for a disciple of Jesus to obey the teachings and example of their master is not a characteristic of a cult or the position of a non-Christian. Salvation through faith and by God's grace does not preclude the following teachings of Jesus and his apostles from being performed (acted upon) by the believer. As the following verses demonstrate (with emphasis added), Jesus surely expected the hearers of his preaching to **do** more than just "have faith" in order to be saved:

> • Every one then who hears these words of mine and **does** them will be like a wise man who built his house upon the rock. (Matthew 7:24, RSV)

---

4. Ibid.

- Why do you call me "Lord, Lord." and not **do** what I tell you? (Luke 6:46)

- If you keep my commandments, you will abide in my love [....] You are my friends if you **do** what I command you. (John 15:10,14)

- And Peter said to them, "**Repent**, and **be baptized** every one of you in the name of Jesus Christ **for the forgiveness of your sins**..." (Acts 2:38)

- But be **doers** of the word, and not hearers only, deceiving yourselves. (James 1:22)

In his article, Slick summarizes Peter's view of baptism as "a representation of the inward reality of regeneration." Yet the very passage that Slick refers to (1 Peter 3:21) clearly states:

And that water is a picture of baptism, **which now saves you**, not by removing dirt from your body, but as a response to God from a clean conscience. (NLT)

It is puzzling that Slick states that "baptism is not necessary for salvation" while the passage he refers us to (1 Peter 3:21) states: "baptism, which now saves you..." If baptism is indeed such a non-essential, as the article asserts, then the Apostle Peter appears to have his facts wrong.

Should we also conclude that Peter is a member of a religious cult, or is a non-Christian, because he states that "baptism saves you"? Peter's words and actions support the Christadelphian position that baptism is a key part of the salvation process taught within the New Testament. I am sure that Christadelphians would want their accusers to notice how every single conversion to the new Christian faith mentioned in the book of Acts was accompanied with water baptism—without exception.

Historically, the Christadelphian position on baptism closely aligns with what can be found in the First London Baptist Confession of Faith, of 1646, which explains:

Baptism is an ordinance of the New Testament, given by Christ, to be dispensed upon persons professing faith, or that are made disciples; who upon profession of faith, ought to be baptized, and after to partake of the Lord's Supper.

Some three and a half centuries later, it is remarkable to see that Christianity has come to the point where a group who holds such a position on baptism is subject to the charge of denying salvation by grace and has become grounds for labeling that group as a non-Christian cult.

Deity of Christ

The other major charge that the CARM article brings against the Christadelphians—a characteristic which purportedly identifies the Christadelphians as a non-Christian cult—is their denial of "the deity of Christ." Unfortunately the article fails to identify where such a phrase can be found in the Bible. For those unfamiliar with the Bible, no such phrase is found within all of Scripture. Also, the article never defines the term. The closest one gets to a definition of "the deity of Christ" is the following:

They [the Christadelphians] deny He [Jesus] is divine in nature. According to John 1:1,14, John 8:58 (with Exodus 3:14), and Col. 2:9, Jesus is God.

Arguably, "divine in nature" isn't much clearer than "deity of Christ" although admittedly "Jesus is God" would at first glance appear pretty straightforward. But just as "deity of Christ" and "divine in nature" are phrases foreign to the Scriptures, so too is the phrase "Jesus is God."

The five Bible references provided by Slick in his claim do not help his cause either, seeing how:

• John 1:1 makes no mention of the name "Jesus" or "Son."

• John 1:14 makes reference to the "word" of God becoming flesh, but it doesn't say anything about a preexistent God named "Jesus" or a "person" named "God the Son" dwelling in heaven, coming to earth and "becoming flesh."

- The "I am" statements found in the Greek of John 8:58 and Exodus 3:14 (LXX) do not match, therefore the assertion that Jesus was claiming to be the God who revealed Himself to Moses at the burning bush is highly dubious. Further, in John 9:9, the man born blind (who Jesus healed) spoke the very same Greek words *ego eimi* ("I am") that Jesus used in John 8:58, yet no one uses this language to claim that the blind man is God.[5]

- The idea found in Colossians 2:9 that in Jesus "the whole fulness of deity dwells bodily" is the same sentiment expressed in Ephesians 3:14–19, where it is found to be the desire of the Apostle Paul for Christians that they too be "filled with deity" (God), just as Jesus was: "… and to know the love of Christ which surpasses knowledge, that you may be filled with **all the fulness of God**."

CARM also fails to show from the Scriptures why such a belief that "Jesus is God" is a prerequisite for being a Christian. Second and third century Christians appear to disagree with CARM's requirement:

In the latter half of the 2d century, Justin Martyr says, "Some there are among ourselves who admit that Jesus is Christ while holding him to be man of men." Still later, Tertullian says, "Common people think of Christ as a man."[6]

---

5. British biblical scholar and Methodist minister, Charles Kingsley Barrett, who was Professor of Divinity at the University of Durham, once commented on John 8:58, saying: "It is not however correct to infer either for the present passage or for the others in which ἐγώ εἰμι [ego eimi] occurs that John wishes to equate Jesus with the supreme God of the Old Testament [....] ἐγώ εἰμι does not identify Jesus with God, but it does draw attention to him in the strongest possible terms. 'I am the one—the one you must look at, and listen to, if you would know God.'" (*The Gospel According to St. John* (Philadelphia: The Westminster Press, 1978), p. 342.) Another Protestant commentator, this one from a 19th century Congregational persuasion, echoes Barrett's sentiment, writing: "Some suppose that, in using the expression, 'I am,' our Lord intended a reference to the divine appellation announced to Moses, 'I am that which I am.' But it is to be remarked that the words of that passage are in the future tense, 'I will be that which I will be;' and most probably it was not intended as a name, but as a declaration of the certain fulfilment of all the promises of God, especially those which related to the deliverance of the Israelites." (John Pye Smith, *The Scripture Testimony of the Messiah*, vol. I (Edinburgh: William Oliphant & Co., 1859), p. 504.)
6. John McClintock and James Strong, "Unitarianism," *Cyclopaedia of Biblical, Theological, and Ecclesiastical Literature*, vol. X, (New York: Harper and Bros., 1886), p. 641.

Also oddly lacking from the CARM article is any reference to the Trinity. Evidently it turns out that belief in the "deity of Christ" is now more important than a belief in the Trinity. Although embraced by mainstream Christianity after the late 4th century, it may come as a surprise to most to learn that neither a belief in "the deity of Christ" nor a belief in the Trinity were characteristics of a *first century* Christian faith.[7]

As several mainstream Christian scholars have confirmed:

- We would be wrong, however, to envision the earliest Christians as somehow thinking in the complex terms of later theology. They did not talk of God as Trinity or refer to Jesus as fully God and fully human.[8]

- The idea of a "Triune God" does not form part of the witness and message of Primitive Christianity.[9]

- All this underlines the point that primitive Christianity did not have an explicit doctrine of the Trinity such as was subsequently elaborated in the creeds of the early church.[10]

- At first the Christian faith was not Trinitarian in the a strictly ontological reference. It was [also] not so in the apostolic and sub-apostolic ages, as reflected in the NT and other early Christian writings. Nor was it so even in the age of the Christian apologists. And even Tertullian, who founded the nomenclature of the ortho-dox doctrine, knew as little of an ontological Trinity as did the apologists; [....][11]

---

7. A reading of the New Testament book of Acts easily confirms this point.
8. Mark D. Roberts, *Jesus Revealed* (Colorado Springs: WaterBrook Press, 2002), p. 133. Roberts is pastor of Irvine Presbyterian Church and adjunct New Testament Professor at Fuller Seminary. He earned degrees in philosophy and religion at Harvard University where he also received his Ph.D. in the New Testament.
9. Emil Brunner, *The Christian Doctrine of God: Dogmatics*, vol. 1, Olive Wyon, trans. (London: Lutterworth Press, 1949), p. 217. Brunner (1889–1966) was the most widely read theologian in the English-speaking world throughout the mid-twentieth century. Brunner was Professor of Systematic and Practical Theology at the University of Zürich from 1924–55.
10. Johannes Schneider, "God," *The New International Dictionary of New Testament Theology*, vol. 2, Colin Brown, ed. (Grand Rapids: Zondervan Publishing House, 1976), p. 84. Schneider (1895–1970), a Baptist, was Chair of New Testament in Berlin University, and Dean of the Faculty of Theology.

- What do we find in the writings of the Christian leaders during roughly the first sixty years of the second century CE? As we might expect, we do not find the developed Trinitarian language or theology that will blossom from the fourth century on. [...] We will be disappointed if we expect to find developed Trinitarian reflection in the early post-apostolic writers. It is simply not there.[12]

- In the immediate post-NT period of the Apostolic Fathers, there were no attempts to speculate about the relationship between God and Christ, Father and Son. [...] The emergence of a trinitarian doctrine [in the fourth century] of God's fatherhood altered what it had meant up to that point. In the Bible and in early creeds and liturgical prayers, God and Father were synonyms.[13]

A First Century Christian Faith

Recall that CARM began their "research" article quite brusquely, asserting:

No, Christadelphianism is not Christian. Like all cults, Christadelphianism denies one or more of the essential doctrines of Christianity.

The Christadelphians would argue that their faith is rooted in the essentials of first century Christianity, which they believe can be summarized thusly:

---

11. William Fulton, "Trinity," *Encyclopedia of Religion and Ethics*, vol. 12, James Hastings, ed. (New York: Charles Scribner's Sons, 1958), p. 461.
12. Roger E. Olson and Christopher A. Hall, *The Trinity* (Grand Rapids: Wm. B. Eerdmans Publ. Co., 2002), pp. 16, 20. Olson is an American Baptist theologian and Professor of Christian Theology of Ethics at the Baylor University. Hall is an American Episcopal theologian who is a leading exponent of paleo-orthodox theology. He was the Chancellor of Eastern University, and the dean of the Templeton Honors College.
13. Catherine Mowry Lacugna, "God," *The HarperCollins Encyclopedia of Catholicism*, Richard McBrien, ed. (New York: HarperCollins, 1995), pp. 567, 9. Lacugna was a feminist Catholic theologian. According to her Wikipedia entry, LaCugna's passion "was to make the doctrine of the Trinity relevant to the everyday life of modern Christians."

- a belief in one God, the God of Israel, as was taught by Jesus when he affirmed the Shema: "And Jesus answered him, The first of all the commandments is, Hear, O Israel; The Lord our God is one Lord" (Mark 12:29, from Deuteronomy 6:4),[14] and where this "one" God is understood to be "the Father," as Jesus himself stated, "Father [....] this is life eternal, that they might know thee the only true God and Jesus Christ whom thou hast sent." (John 17:1,3, RSV)

- a recognition that Jesus of Nazareth was the Messiah/Christ (promised, anointed future king of Israel)[15] as John stresses at the end of his gospel account, "these [things] are written, that ye might believe that Jesus *is the Christ, the Son of God;*[16] and that believing ye might have life through his name" (John 20:31)

- a belief that Jesus died on account of the sins of his brethren, and not on account of any personal wrong-doing of his own, and that he was raised bodily from the dead (1 Corinthians 15:3–4)

- a belief that Jesus was the "prophet like unto Moses" that God would raise up from among the Israelites, from the seed of Abraham, who spoke God's word, and would fulfill the promises made to Abraham (that in him all nations of the earth would be blessed); and that this One would reign as king over the house of Jacob, on the throne of David (over a redeemed Israel) and eventually over all nations (Deuteronomy 18:15, Luke 1:32–33, Galatians 3:8)

- a belief that God raised Jesus from the dead and exalted him to the right hand of the throne of God (Acts 2:32–33)

- a belief that Jesus was the judge appointed by God to judge the living and dead (Acts 10:42, Romans 14:9)

---

14. The Shema, so called from the first word of Deuteronomy 6:4-6, שמע, i.e. *hear,* occurring in one of the key prayers of the Jewish ritual, is a kind of confession of faith that every devout Israelite is to repeat morning and evening, and is a touchstone of monotheism that uniquely distinguished Judaism from other faiths.
15. See Peter's confession of faith in Matthew 16:16–18, a statement of faith which Jesus described as the "rock" or foundation of the Christian Church.
16. For a discussion on the meaning of the title "Son of God" see pages 78–79.

• a belief that salvation and the restoration of God's kingdom on earth will come about through the agency of Jesus reigning as king over the nation of Israel (Luke 1:32–33, Acts 1:6)

These were the common beliefs of a first century Christian according to the Bible. These have also been the beliefs of the Christadelphians from their beginning—for more than a century and a half. Notwithstanding these facts, the CARM article rejects the possibility that the Christadelphians are genuine Christians, describing them instead as "a false religion. It is definitely not Christian."

The Mud-Slinging Continues

The article also goes on to make several other misrepresentations, mixed in with misunderstandings, stating:

In regards to Jesus, it ["Christadelphianism"] teaches that [....]

• Jesus had a sinful nature

• Jesus needed salvation[17]

[...] they are saying that Jesus Himself also needed to be saved.

With respect to the first charge (i.e., that Jesus had a sinful nature), the Christadelphian position is misrepresented. Christadelphians believe that the New Testament depicts Jesus as experiencing temptation in the very same way that you and I experience temptation. It is not that "Jesus had a sinful nature," as Slick inaccurately reports, but rather, as Hebrews states:

Therefore he [Jesus] had to be made like his brethren **in every respect**, so that he might become a merciful and faithful high priest in the service of God, to make expiation for the sins of the people. For because he himself has suffered and been tempted, he is able to help those who are tempted. (Hebrews 2:17–18, RSV)[18]

---

17. Slick, ibid.

In making the charge that the Christadelphians teach that "Jesus had a sinful nature," Slick included a bibliographic reference to a Christadelphian book titled *The Christadelphians, What They Believe and Preach*. Although he was kind enough to include the page number, Slick failed to quote a single line from this source. To illustrate how Slick has incorrectly summarized the Christadelphian position, I will share from the book the page content he had to work with:

> Therefore, we conclude that it is not only that Jesus was called a sinner at his trial by his enemies or that he was "numbered with the transgressors" when he was crucified between two thieves, but more particularly that he shared the very nature which had made a sinner out of every other man who had borne it. It is for this reason that the nature we bear is called "sinful flesh" or more briefly, "sin" (Romans 7:20 and 8:4). The source of our temptations, in simple Bible shorthand, is itself called "sinful" or "sin", even though we are in no way blamed for possessing the nature we bear. Christ was "made sin" for us by sharing our human nature and, though sinless, by being treated as a sinner by sinful men. He "knew no sin" because he never sinned, but not because he was never tempted.
>
> In order to bind sin and take it captive, Jesus met it on its own ground, human nature. Thus his victory was both true and unique. True in that he overcame sin though tempted precisely as we are; and unique in that he is the only one who has been totally sinless even though tempted. Christ did not demonstrate righteousness and holiness in a detached way; he brought his sinless life to God in this earthen vessel of human nature.[19]

---

18. The very fact that the Bible describes Jesus as being capable of temptation works against Slick's claim that "Jesus is God," for the Bible also states that, "**God cannot be tempted with evil** and he himself tempts no one; but each person is tempted when he is lured and enticed by his own desire," (James 1:13–14). The Christadelphian would argue that because God cannot be tempted with evil and yet the Gospel narratives describe Jesus as being tempted in the wilderness shortly after his baptism, Jesus therefore could not possibly be God as Slick doggedly insists. Their logic appears simple and can be reworded thusly: Jesus was tempted with evil; God cannot be tempted with evil; ergo, Jesus is not God.

So I ask the reader, is the above Christadelphian position accurately represented by Slick's charge that Christadelphians teach that "Jesus had a sinful nature"?

The Christadelphian view is made even clearer by the nineteenth century Swiss Protestant theologian Frédéric Louis Godet, chaplain to the Prince Royal of Prussia, William I, and professor of theology at Neuchâtel, who once wrote:

> How could we assign any serious meaning to the moral struggles in the history of Jesus—the temptation, for example,—if His perfect holiness was the necessary consequence of His miraculous birth? But it is not so. The miraculous birth was only the *negative* condition of the spotless holiness of Jesus. Entering into human life in this way, He was placed in the normal condition of man before his fall, and put in a position to fulfil the career originally set before man, in which he was to advance from innocence to holiness. He was simply freed from the obstacle which, owing to the way in which we are born, hinders us from accomplishing this task. But in order to change this possibility into a reality, Jesus had to exert every instant His own free will, and to devote Himself continually to the service of good and the fulfilment of the task assigned Him, namely, "the keeping of His Father's commandment." His miraculous birth, therefore, in no way prevented this conflict from being real. It gave Him liberty *not to sin*, but did not take away from Him the liberty of sinning.[20]

Now with respect to Slick's charge that Christadelphians teach that "Jesus needed salvation," a return to the book of Hebrews will assist us in understanding what way the Christadelphians understand Jesus was in need of salvation:

> In the days of his flesh, Jesus offered up prayers and supplications, with loud cries and tears, to him who was able **to save**

---

19. Harry Tennant, *The Christadelphians, What They Believe and Preach* (Birmingham: The Christadelphian, 1986), p. 74.
20. Frédéric Louis Godet, *A Commentary on the Gospel of St. Luke*, vol. 1, E. W. Shalders, transl. (Edinburgh: T. & T. Clark, 1889), p. 94.

him from death, and he was heard for his godly fear. (Hebrews 5:7, RSV)

He entered once for all into the Holy Place, taking not the blood of goats and calves but **his own blood, thus securing an eternal redemption**. (Hebrews 9:12, RSV)

Additionally, Jesus in Gethsemane offered up prayers for his deliverance (salvation) to the one God who could save him from the cruel fate of death on a cross:

He advanced a little and fell prostrate in prayer, saying, "My Father, if it is possible, let this cup pass from me; yet, not as I will, but as you will." (Matthew 26:39, NAB)

Christadelphians hold strongly to the belief that Jesus was mortal, in contrast to the belief that Jesus was an immortal "person" from another realm who simply appeared to have died. Christadelphians teach that Jesus, like his brethren, was not only subject to temptation, but also subject to suffering and ultimately death. These things—the desires and weaknesses of his flesh—needed to be defeated, and the shackles of mortality needed to be removed. His mortality needed to be "swallowed up in victory," as the Bible describes the hope of mortal man (1 Corinthians 15:54). Or as one editor of a major Christadelphian periodical concisely explained:

[...] Jesus never yielded to any impulse to disobey God; he was always obedient; whereas all others had become servants to the flesh he was servant to God. Sin had been obeyed by all others, but Sin could establish no claim over Jesus. He shared our mortality and our temptations; he inherited the effects of sin in Eden at the beginning of the race as we all do. In the first Adam Sin triumphed; in the last Adam it was vanquished [....][21]

---

21. John Carter, "Words and Meanings," *The Christadelphian*, vol. 95, February 1958, p. 83.

It is in this sense that Christadelphians believe Jesus needed salvation: to be freed from the mortality inherent to humanity. This is how he benefited from his own death after being raised by God from the dead, never to die again.

Yet, Slick asserts:

This is absolutely unbiblical and heretical and needs to be labeled for what it is: false doctrine. [...] The Christadelphian religion is a false religion. It is definitely not Christian. This is not to say that there are not decent people who intend to serve God honestly and truthfully. But sincerity does not bridge the gap between God and man. Only the blood of the real Jesus does that, not a false Christ with a sin nature who himself needed salvation.[22]

It is hard to know whether the "researcher" simply misunderstands the Christadelphian position or whether he is intentionally misrepresenting it. Again, the Christadelphians take the position that Jesus was like us in every way, meaning that he was capable of being tempted to sin. This is not the same thing as being "sinful." Teaching that Jesus was mortal and subject to the desires and weaknesses of the flesh and that he experienced temptation (yet never sinned)—which is the Christadelphian position—is not the same thing as believing Jesus was "sinful." "Sinful" implies "being full of sin"—implying that Jesus was a habitual sinner—an interpretation that Slick perhaps wants the reader to think is the Christadelphian position so as to be able to deliver a verbal death blow to what he views a "false religion." However this is an error on his part, or a failing to understand the ways in which Jesus was "made like his brethren in every respect" with regard to temptation and death.

Slick continues his article by quoting 1 John 4:2-3 with the hope that the reader will perceive that Christadelphians are "anti-Christ," and that they, as he asserts, "cannot have the true Jesus and are, therefore, serving a false God":[23]

22. Slick, ibid.
23. Ibid.

By this you know the Spirit of God: every spirit that confesses that Jesus Christ has come in the flesh is from God; and every spirit that does not confess Jesus is not from God; and this is the spirit of the antichrist, of which you have heard that it is coming, and now it is already in the world.

Slick wants the reader to interpret the phrase "Christ has come in the flesh" in this Bible passage as meaning something along the lines of: *"God the Son, the second person of the Trinity, a tri-personal perfect being, though preexisting from eternity as God, descended to earth in the form of an embryo, took up residence in Mary's womb and was sustained by her for nine months, was ultimately born as a man child, grew up in the wisdom and favor of God and who by nature was incapable of sinning, eventually died on a cross after calling upon God to save him from death, all the while being the immortal God."* Whether this makes sense or not is not important. This is simply how we are expected to understand "come in the flesh," and if anyone fails to do so, they are in jeopardy of being labeled as "anti-Christ." Yet, there is more than one way to understand the phrase "come in the flesh," as even orthodox Catholic and Protestant scholars acknowledge, as in the following:

• 1 John 5:6 shows that the confession of [1 John] 4:2, "Jesus Christ having come in flesh," probably signifies for the author and his readers something like, "Jesus Christ having acted salvifically with the instrumentality of (his) flesh." Taken together, the three insights gained from 5:6 suggest as a working hypothesis that the confession of Jesus Christ *en sarki elēlythota* [*having come in the flesh*] in 4:2 [...] **is most probably another way of speaking about Jesus Christ's death**, since, as 5:6 indicates most clearly, the author and the secessionists have parted company over one basic issue: the theological relevance of the death of Jesus Christ.[24] [emphasis added]

• The confession of "Jesus Christ having come in (the) flesh" (1 John 4:2; cf. 2 John 7) is the author's way of speaking about the death of

---

24. Martinus C. de Boer, "The Death of Jesus Christ and His Coming in the Flesh," *Novum Testamentum*, vol. 33 (October 1991), p. 340.

Jesus Christ and it would have been so understood by the first readers.[25]

- It must be noted that the author says "come in the flesh," not "come into the flesh," and so **the act of incarnation is not the point.** [emphasis added][26]

- Remark that S. John does not say 'come *into* the flesh', but '*in* the flesh': Christ did not descend (as Cerinthus said) into an already existing man, but He came in human nature; [....][27]

And, of course, "human nature" implies being susceptible to temptation and death. These are not attributes of an angel, let alone of an Almighty, Eternal God[28]—whom Slick here has equated with Jesus.

Using 1 John 4:2-3 to condemn others, calling them "anti-Christ," "heretical," teaching "false doctrine" and "serving a false God" is a dangerous practice. One needs to be very careful when playing the role of "heresy hunter," as this example illustrates.

Un-Christian or Un-Orthodox?

It is not my desire to go on refuting each of the inaccuracies and misrepresentations that CARM's online article puts forward. The purpose of this chapter is not to defend the Christadelphians, per se, but rather this chapter serves to illustrate with a real-life example the palpable hostility that can be found among mainstream Christians against the Christadelphians, and to document how common it is for their adversaries to bring forth invalid arguments, false statements, and misrepresentations when describing Christadelphian doctrines to the public. From this example we can see that the dispute mainstream Christianity has against the Christadelphians is not about their behavior or practices,

---

25. Ibid., p. 345.
26. Raymond E. Brown, *The Epistles of John* (Anchor Yale Bible) (New York: Doubleday, 1982), p. 493.
27. Alfred Plummer, *The Cambridge Bible for Schools and Colleges: The Epistles of S. John* (Cambridge: University Press, 1906), p. 142.
28. James 1:13-14.

but rather it is one that might be classified as "an unhealthy interest in controversies and quarrels about words that result in envy, strife, malicious talk, evil suspicions" (1 Timothy 6:4, NIV). In some sense I am getting ahead of myself, for this online example draws us ever nearer to the realization that there is only one reason why their critics label Christadelphians a "cult"—which I will address in more detail in the next chapter.

For now, let me conclude that although the "research ministry" at CARM failed to substantiate the charge that "Christadelphianism is not Christian," the organization did at least succeed in highlighting some of the differences between mainstream/"orthodox" Christianity and the Christadelphians. In this, they are correct: the Christadelphians are indeed *un*orthodox by modern mainstream standards. But the question still remains, does this make the Christadelphians a non-Christian cult?[29]

---

29. Interestingly, Matt Slick, who posted his "research" originally in 2002, removed his work from the Internet sometime after 2020. An archived copy can be found at: web.archive.org/web/20200924213809/https://carm.org/is-christadelphianism-christian

CHAPTER 4

Unorthodoxy

At any given moment there is an orthodoxy, a body of ideas of which it is assumed that all right-thinking people will accept without question.... Anyone who challenges the prevailing orthodoxy finds himself silenced with surprising effectiveness. A genuinely unfashionable opinion is almost never given a fair hearing....[1]

—GEORGE ORWELL

THE LIBERAL FREE-THINKING organization Religious Tolerance (religioustolerance.org) describes the theological beliefs of the Christadelphians as being "much closer to those of the original Christian movement—the Jewish Christian church founded by Jesus' followers and centered in Jerusalem under the leadership of James—than it is to most current Christian faith groups."[2] Such an impartial assessment, if true, is a serious threat to Protestants who believe that such an honor belongs to them, not to some 19th-century emergent, non-conforming "cult."[3] While Christadelphians do not conform to the creeds which have defined Christianity from the 4th century onward, the fact is that non-conformity to extra-biblical creeds, such as the Nicæan and Athanasian Creeds, is not a biblical or rational reason to label a group as non-Christian or a cult.

---

1. "The Freedom of the Press." Unused preface to George Orwell "Animal Farm" (August 17, 1945), first published in "The Times Literary Supplement," September 15, 1972.
2. B. A. Robinson, "About the Christadelphians: 1848 to Now," http://www.religioustolerance.org/chr_delp.htm, retrieved July 24, 2022.
3. Because of the ambiguity and baggage that comes with the "Protestant" label, Christadelphians generally do not view themselves as such, but rather as restorationists. Restorationism is the belief that Christianity should be restored along the lines of what is known about the apostolic early church, which restorationists see as the search for a purer form of the religion.

Down through the ages almost all non-conformist groups were small in size, spoken ill of, and ostracized by the established church and therefore by society in general. If we were to identify a cult based solely upon a group's minority status and its non-conformity to the status quo, well then the first century Christians would have unquestionably qualified as a cult! Even the reformers of the 16th century—Luther, Calvin, Zwingli and others—appeared outrageous to the majority of the population in their day. Each reformer was standing apart for reasons of conscience, usually based on their understanding of the Bible. And this is what the Christadelphians believe they are doing: standing apart from mainstream Christianity for conscience sake, based upon their understanding of the Bible. Christadelphians strive for a return to a first century faith, not a faith influenced and defined by tradition or prescribed by councils and creeds of the 4th and latter centuries, enforced through threats of violence by the State, as was the case with the doctrine of the Trinity, along with other doctrines.

Back to the Cult Question

As we've seen, the Christadelphians are not branded as a "cult" by their detractors on account of their behavior, their organization, their history, or the role of prominent Christadelphians past or present. The Christadelphians fail to meet any of the twenty-three previously mentioned behavior traits that are commonly used these days (rightly or wrongly) to identify a religious cult.[4] Why then do other Christians describe the Christadelphians as a cult or as non-Christian? The answer is due to one remaining characteristic—one which was alluded to in the previous chapter, and which we will look at in more detail in the next two chapters—that is, Christadelphians are labeled as a "cult" due to the different views that they hold on biblical doctrine when compared with mainstream Catholic and Protestant traditions.

On the back cover of this book the reader will find the current definition for the noun *cult* in the *Oxford English Dictionary.* Among its multiple definitions is the following:

---

4. See Chapter 2.

2. a relatively small group of people having religious beliefs or practices regarded by others as strange or as imposing excessive control over members

As we've already covered in Chapter 2, members within the Christadelphian community are not carefully managed, constantly monitored, or manipulated through peer pressure, nor are they kept "in line" through the threat or use of punishment (material, social, and emotional). Consequently, the second half of this definition is not applicable to the Christadelphians. It is the first half which comes the closest to finding application to the Christadelphians:

2. a relatively *small* group of people having religious *beliefs* or practices *regarded by others as strange* . . . . [emphasis added].

Unquestionably, the Christadelphians are "small," with their numbers estimated to be between 50000-60000 worldwide. But that fact alone doesn't justify labeling this group as a cult. The early Christians were a small band, too, but modern, mainstream Christians don't brand them with the epithet of "cult."

This leaves the reference to "having religious beliefs or practices regarded by others as strange" as the only element that could apply to this group. With respect to "practices," however, we come up short again, for as previously observed, the Christadelphians have no worship practices that mainstream Christians might deem as "strange." Thus we're left with nothing else but the realm of "religious beliefs."

In his book, *Unmasking the Cults*, Alan W. Gomes presents a long list of characteristics which he believes are common to a cult. However, in his opening chapter, Gomes provides what he calls "the Preferred Definition of a Cult," which he describes as:

A cult of Christianity is a group of people who claim to be Christian, yet embrace a particular doctrinal system taught by an individual leader, group of leaders, or organization, which (system) denies (either explicitly or implicitly) one or more of the central doctrines of the Christian faith as taught in the sixty-six books of the Bible.[5]

Gomes' "preferred" identifier of a Christian cult, simply put, is when a Christian minority rejects an opinion[6] that the majority believes is central to the Christian faith. However, this definition is fraught with problems. For example, as we've already suggested, applying such a definition at the beginning of the 16th century would have classified the Protestant Reformation movement as a religious cult! Is holding to an unorthodox belief really a sufficient reason to classify someone as belonging to a cult?

And this is what it comes down to when other Christians label the Christadelphians a cult. They do not earn the opprobrium on account of any aberrant behavior. They are not pejoratively labeled due to an authoritarian leader exercising high control of their members. Instead, because Christadelphians reject at least one doctrine which the current majority of Christians (or Christian clergy) view as a fundamental Bible truth, for this reason alone are they marked as a cult. Under Gomes' "preferred" definition, all it takes is for them to reject one mainstream belief—the embracing of an alternative interpretation with respect to a perceived essential doctrine of the Christian faith—to earn them the scarlet "C." Consequently, Christadelphians can now be labeled with the same pejorative term that is used to describe the Order of the Solar Temple, the Branch Davidians, and the followers of Jim Jones—groups who committed murder and mass suicide—simply because they interpret certain Bible passages differently from the mainstream.

Simply a minority-held interpretation of certain Bible texts can qualify a group as a Christian cult. This is where we are today, like it or not.

So, having pinpointed why the term *cult* has been used in association with the Christadelphians, let's now look at the specifics. What are the particular doctrines and Scriptural interpretations that make the Christadelphians stand out as being unorthodox in the sight of mainstream Christianity?

---

5. Alan W. Gomes, *Unmasking the Cults* (Grand Rapids: Zondervan, 1995), p. 7.

6. In Greek, the word *orthos* means "straight" or "true" and *doxa*, means "an opinion." *Unorthodoxy* therefore means "not having the correct opinion or point of view."

At the Heart of the Controversy

The primary doctrines where Christadelphians disagree with mainstream Christianity and which lie at the heart of the controversy between them and the mainstream are the following:

- the state of the dead and future reward/punishment of the righteous and wicked
- the identity of God and Jesus

In the next two chapters we will look at these doctrines in more detail.

CHAPTER 5

Conditional Immortality

Death is the final stage of growth in this life. There is no total death. Only the body dies. The self or the spirit, or whatever you may wish to label it, is eternal. You may interpret this in any way that makes you comfortable.[1]

—ELISABETH KUBLER-ROSS

These were all commended for their faith, yet none of them received what had been promised. God had planned something better for us so that only together with us would they be made perfect.

—HEBREWS 11:39–40, NIV

THE FIRST LIE ever told in the Bible was expressed in the words of the serpent to the woman: "Surely you will not die" (Genesis 3:4, NET). Yet the first woman died, as did her husband, Adam, and so also followed all their children to the grave. And we too will one day die, unpleasant as the thought is.[2] Which explains why we don't want to think much about the subject of death, even though death like a shadow follows wherever we go. We may try to ignore this dark subject, but we cannot hide from it, or from the truth subsequently revealed by God to Adam and Eve that, "for you are dust, and to dust you will return," (Genesis 3:19).

Christian scholar James Payton called our mortality a "cosmic disease,"[3] and it is. But it is also part of God's solution to an even greater disease: sin. In our present sinful condition, immortality of any sort

---

1. *Death: The Final Stage* (New York: Touchstone, 1986), p. 166.
2. The only exception is for those who are alive at the return of Jesus, (see 1 Thess. 4:15–17.)
3. James R. Payton, *Light from the Christian East* (Downers Grove: InterVarsity Press, 2007), p. 111. "...humanity suffers, ever since Adam and Eve, from the 'cosmic disease' of death."

would be disastrous, which explains why God intervened in the Garden of Eden, announcing, "Now that the man has become like one of us, knowing good and evil, he must not be allowed to stretch out his hand and take also from the tree of life and eat, and live forever," (Genesis 3:22). In the Genesis narrative, God then drove Adam and his wife from the Garden cutting off access to the Tree of Life, which, by God's grace, had been available up until the Fall. Consequently, their right to "live forever" was removed, and with time, Adam and Eve, and their descendants, died and returned to the dust from which they were created.

But, as noted previously, before they were banished, God informed the couple of a simple truth: "By the sweat of your brow you will eat food until you return to the ground, for out of it you were taken; for you are dust, and to dust you will return," (Genesis 3:19). Though God spoke plainly that mankind would return to dust, most Christians prefer to believe something "higher and nobler," more akin to the words of the serpent, who said to the woman, "Surely you will not die," (Genesis 3:4).

Plato taught that "the soul of man is immortal and imperishable."[4] The idea that some spark of intelligence within us, some element of consciousness or existence of being continues after our death is a belief held by both Christians and non-Christians. "Death is simply a shedding of the physical body like the butterfly shedding its cocoon. It is a transition to a higher state of consciousness where you continue to perceive, to understand, to laugh, and to be able to grow," suggested Elisabeth Kübler-Ross.[5] Many imagine that, to some degree, immortality is everyone's birthright.

Yet such an idea has never been explicitly taught in the Bible. And when it comes to the Christadelphians, such an idea is flatly rejected—and they bring forth many reasons.

Attached to most Christadelphian statements of faith is found a list of "Doctrines To Be Rejected," among which include:

4. Plato, "The Republic," *The Dialogues of Plato*, vol. II, B. Jowett, ed. (New York: Bigelow, Brown & Co., Inc., 1914), p. 398.
5. Elisabeth Kübler-Ross, "Death Does Not Exist," *We Shall be Heard: Women Speakers in America*, P. Kennedy and G. Shields, eds. (Belmont: Wadsworth Publishing, 1998), p. 348. Kübler-Ross was a psychologist and served on the Association for Near-Death Studies.

We reject the doctrine of: The Immortality of the Soul
We believe: That the immortality of the soul is a pagan fiction, subversive of the first law of the Deity's moral government, viz., that the wages of sin is death.

We reject the doctrine of: The Theory of Disembodied Existence
We believe: That there is no existence in death, conscious or unconscious, and that the popular belief in heaven and hell is a delusion. Therefore —
A. That the wicked will not suffer eternal torture, but will be engulfed in total destruction after resurrection.
B. That the righteous will not ascend to kingdoms beyond the skies at death, or at any other time, but will inherit the earth forever.[6]

The Christadelphians claim that the philosophical idea of an immortal soul has more in common with the Greek philosopher Plato than with the writings of Moses, the prophets, the apostles, and the teachings of Jesus. Plato believed in the existence of an immortal "soul" or conscious life essence, which was freed upon death.[7] Plato suggested that immortality was an innate endowment from our Creator, rather than something that our Creator prevented us from obtaining on account of sin. Many influential Christians have chosen to believe in Plato's version of human anthropology, such as John Calvin, John Wesley, and numerous other theologians, including Augustine.

In contrast, Christadelphians believe that man returns to the dust of the earth when he dies, while figuratively his breath (of life) returns to "the God who gives breath to all creatures" (Numbers 16:22, NLT). There is nothing unique in the breath (sometimes translated as "the spirit") of man when compared with that of animals, as the Preacher explains:

For the fate of the children of Adam and the fate of animals is the same. As one dies, so dies the other; they all have the same breath. (Ecclesiastes 3:19, CSB)

---

6. William Alexander Curtis, *A History of Creeds and Confessions of Faith in Christendom and Beyond* (Edinburgh: T. & T. Clark, 1911), p. 314.
7. See Plato's *Phædon: or a Dialogue on the Immortality of the Soul.*

The Influence of Greek Thought on Christianity

As introduced above, Christadelphians take the position that the doctrine of the resurrection of the dead has been displaced within mainstream Christianity by the belief in the immortality of the soul. Christadelphians believe that Plato's theory was overlaid with Christian sentiment and is now so widely accepted that few think twice about questioning its presuppositions. Dr. Laidlaw, a professor and minister within the Scottish Free Churches, in his *Bible Doctrine of Man* says that "gradually, in Christian schools, the Greek influence prevailed, and even in the Christian church the idea of the soul's immortality for long[8] took the place of the Scripture doctrine of a future life."[9]

The Biblical Foundation of Conditional Immortality

Christadelphians, in contrast, are among those who hold a view of death known as "conditional immortality." Conditionalists maintain that mankind is totally unconscious in the death state, that he ceases to exist other than in whatever decompositional elements remain when the person returns to dust, and that immortality is a future reward to be granted unto only a faithful collective when Jesus returns.

Such a view, if true, poses a serious problem to the Catholic teaching of conscious, immaterial "souls" or "spirits" departing the body and immediately being carried off to heaven, purgatory, or a place of torment. Conditional immortality, if true, undermines the validity of praying to the Virgin Mary and a multitude of saints, for all of these would be dead and thus non-existent intercessors. Conditional immortality also challenges a great block of evangelical Protestant churches which have traditionally used images of eternal fire awaiting the lost when they die in order to "encourage" (scare?) potential converts into accepting Jesus as their "personal savior." These "altar calls" are often presented as a means by which a person can obtain assurance that if they were to die that day, their "soul" would be transported to heaven to be with Jesus.[10]

---

8. That is, "for a long time...."
9. John Laidlaw, *The Bible Doctrine of Man, Or, The Anthropology and Psychology of Scripture* (Edinburgh: T. & T. Clark, 1895), p. 318.

If the Christadelphians are correct about the intermediate state—that we utterly die and that no part of a person ascends consciously into heaven—then many Evangelicals are left with a fiction at the heart of their "gospel message."

In the New Testament, one cannot find such "altar calls" or the use of similar scare tactics by Jesus and his disciples. Throughout the Gospels, without any exception, Jesus unambiguously taught that the righteous dead will be rewarded at the resurrection of the dead, *at his return*, not immediately upon their death. For example:

- "For the Son of man is to come with his angels in the glory of his Father, and then he will repay every man for what he has done." (Matthew 16:27, RSV)

- "When the Son of man comes in his glory, and all the angels with him, then he will sit on his glorious throne. Before him will be gathered all the nations, and he will separate them one from another as a shepherd separates the sheep from the goats, and he will place the sheep at his right hand, but the goats at the left. Then the King will say to those at his right hand, 'Come, O blessed of my Father, inherit the kingdom prepared for you from the foundation of the world;'" (Matthew 25:31–34, RSV)

- "...and you will be blessed, because they cannot repay you. You will be repaid at the resurrection of the just." (Luke 14:14, RSV)

- "...but those who are accounted worthy to attain to that age and to the resurrection from the dead neither marry nor are given in marriage." (Luke 20:35, RSV)

- "Do not marvel at this; for the hour is coming when all who are in the tombs will hear his voice and come forth, those who have done good, to the resurrection of life, and those

---

10. These days it appears that more and more that pastors are dropping the hell fire eternal torment imagery and instead replacing it with a warning of "eternal separation from God" as the result of rejecting Jesus—a fate a bit more ambiguous, a pinch less terrifying, and a description closer to reality.

who have done evil, to the resurrection of judgment." (John 5:28–29)[11]

The Old Testament describes the death state in these terms:

- "Dust thou art, and unto dust shalt thou return." (Genesis 3:19, KJV)[12]

- "Why did I not die at birth, come forth from the womb and expire? [...] For then I should have lain down and been quiet; I should have slept; then I should have been at rest, with kings and counselors of the earth who rebuilt ruins for themselves, [...] Or why was I not as a hidden untimely birth, as infants that never see the light? There the wicked cease from troubling, and there the weary are at rest." (Job 3:11,13–14,16–17, RSV)

- "For in death there is no remembrance of thee: in the grave who shall give thee thanks?" (Psalms 6:5, KJV)

- "Let the wicked be ashamed, and let them be silent in the grave." (Psalms 31:17, KJV)

- "The dead praise not the LORD, neither any that go down into silence." (Psalms 115:17, KJV)

- [As for man] "When his breath departs he returns to his earth; on that very day his plans perish." (Psalms 146:4, RSV)

---

11. Additional references that describe rewards and judgment taking place at Jesus' return and not at the moment of death, include Matthew 13:36–49, Mark 10:30, John 14:3, 1 Corinthians 4:5, 15:51-54, 2 Corinthians 4:14, Philippians 3:10–11, Colossians 3:4, 2 Thessalonians 1:7,10, 2 Timothy 4:8, Hebrews 9:28, 11:35, 1 Peter 5:4, 1 John 3:2.

12. Was God speaking here to Adam's *body*, or was he speaking to the *whole Adam*? If God was talking to Adam's body, then it appears that God's curse upon mankind completely overlooked the "real" and essential Adam, for no further elucidation on Adam's punishment beyond these words are to be found. There are no words concerning the fate of Adam's "eternal soul" or "essential spark" in the curse pronounced by God in Genesis 3.

- "For the living know that they will die, but the dead know nothing [...] Their love and their hate and their envy have already perished [....]" (Ecclesiastes 9:5–6, RSV).

- "There is no work, nor device, nor knowledge, nor wisdom, in the grave, whither thou goest." (Ecclesiastes 9:10, KJV)

- "For the grave cannot praise thee, death can not celebrate thee: they that go down into the pit cannot hope for thy truth." (Isaiah 38:18, KJV)

Worth Considering

In addition to the above verses which support their position, the Christadelphians would also want their critics to consider the following:

- In 1513, Pope Leo X issued a bull (*Apostoloici regimis*) declaring: "We do condemn and reprobate all who assert that the intelligent soul is mortal." This was directed against the growing threat to the Catholic Church from those who denied the popular belief in the natural immortality of the soul. With the advent of the printing press and the translation of the Bible into vulgar tongues by Wycliffe, Luther, and Tyndale, the belief in the conditional immortality of man increased significantly. Conditional immortality, if it were true, would totally uproot a Catholic system which relied greatly on the intercession of Mary and dead saints and the use of indulgences to shorten a person's stay in purgatory. For the welfare of Roman Catholicism, belief in the absolute mortality of man had to be expunged and those who held such a view anathematized.

- In 1517, Martin Luther posted his 95 Theses to the church door at Wittenberg, accusing the Catholic church of heresy upon heresy. Three years later, Luther published a more detailed defense of 41 of those original 95 theses. In this latter work, Luther decried the pope's immortality declaration of 1513 (see immediately above). Luther's 27th proposition read: "I permit the Pope to establish articles of faith for himself and for his own faithful—such are: That the bread and wine are transubstantiated in the sacrament; ... *that the soul is immortal*; and all these endless monstrosities in the Roman dunghill of decretals...."[13] Francis Blackburne, an 18th century archbishop of the Church of England, wrote concerning Luther's position that the state of the dead is that of unconsciousness, that "Luther espoused the doctrine of the sleep of the soul, upon a Scripture foundation, and then he made use of it as a confutation of purgatory, and saint worship, and continued in that belief to the last moment of his life."[14]

Paul Althaus (1888-1966), the leading Luther historian and theologian of his day, wrote even more clearly concerning Luther's views of the intermediate state: "Luther generally understands the condition between death and the resurrection as a deep and dreamless sleep without consciousness and feeling. When the dead are awakened on the Last Day, they will—like a man who wakes up in the morning—know neither where they were nor how long they have rested. [Luther wrote] 'For just as a man who falls asleep and sleeps soundly until morning does not know what has happened to him when he wakes up, so we shall suddenly rise on the Last Day; and we shall know neither what death has been like or how we have come through it.' Luther therefore says nothing about souls without their bodies enjoying true life and blessedness before the resurrection. They sleep in 'the peace of Christ.'"[15]

Luther, in his commentary on Ecclesiastes 9:5-6, wrote:

---

13. Martin Luther, *Assertio Omnium Articulorum M. Lutheri per Bullam Leonis X. Novissimam Damnatorum* (Assertion of all the articles of M. Luther condemned by the latest Bull of Leo X.), article 27, Weimar edition of *Luther's Works*, Vol. 7, pp. 131-2, emphasis added.

14. Francis Blackbourne, *Short Historical View of the Controversy Concerning an Intermediate State* (London: T. Field, 1765), p. 14.

15. Paul Althaus, *The Theology of Martin Luther* (Philadelphia: Fortress Press, 1966), pp. 414-5.

"The living, he [Solomon] says, know that they will die, and therefore in life they use this hope. [...] *But the dead know nothing, and they have no more reward.* Jerome has clumsily distorted this passage to apply to the reward of the dead in purgatory. Solomon seems to feel that the dead are asleep in such a way that they know nothing whatever. And I do not believe that there is a more powerful passage in Scripture to show that the dead are asleep and do not know anything about our affairs—this in opposition to the invocation of the saints and the fiction of purgatory."[16]

- William Tyndale (1484–1536), martyr, and translator of the first printed edition of the English Bible, like Luther, opposed Pope Leo's bull with regard to the immortality of the soul. In writing to Thomas More, the pope's champion in England at that time, Tyndale argued, "And ye [Catholics], in putting them [the departed souls] in heaven, hell, and purgatory, [ye] destroy the arguments wherewith Christ and Paul prove the resurrection [of the righteous]... And again, if the souls be in heaven, tell me why they be not in as good case as the angels be? And then what cause [usefulness] is there of the resurrection?"[17] Tyndale recognized how the biblical hope of the resurrection of the dead is in conflict with the popular belief that the dead are judged through a transmutation of an invisible, immaterial soul which is rewarded (or punished) immediately upon death. If the dead receive their reward when their souls immediately flit off to heaven to enjoy eternal bliss, then a future resurrection of one's body is of little importance. Away with it!

Although Tyndale did not mention it in his debate with Thomas More, the belief that the righteous dead make their way into a celestial realm of felicity would appear to nullify the need for Jesus to die as the savior of mankind. For if

---

16. Martin Luther, *Luther's Works*, vol. 15, Jaroslav Pelikan, ed. (St. Louis: Concordia Pub., 1972), p. 147, emphasis added.

17. William Tyndale, *An Answer to Sir Thomas More's Dialogue*, Parker's 1850 reprint, Bk. 4, ch. 4, pp. 180–1.

Abel, Abraham, Moses, and Job all found themselves in heaven after they died, then Jesus' sacrifice is not as important as one might think, seeing how individuals could obtain heaven/eternal life without the death of Jesus.

- William Temple (1881–1944), serving as Anglican Archbishop of York and then later of Canterbury, wrote: "But one thing we can say with confidence: everlasting torment is to be ruled out. If men had not imported the Greek and unbiblical notion of the natural indestructibility of the individual soul, and then read the New Testament with that already in their minds, they would have drawn from it a belief, not in everlasting torment, but in annihilation. It is the fire that is called æonian (eternal), not the life cast into it."[18]

- John Wycliffe, Michael Sattler (martyr), John Milton, Isaac Newton, Dr. Joseph Priestley, Dean Henry Alford, Henry Constable, Franz Delitzsch, F. F. Bruce, and John Stott are just a tiny sampling of additional theologians who have rejected the Catholic and mainstream Protestant view of the soul's immortality and avowed the scripturalness of conditional immortality.

- In 1995, an officially appointed Church of England commission on doctrine rejected the idea of hell as a place of fire, pitchforks and screams of unending agony, describing it instead as a future place of annihilation for all who reject the love of God.[19]

- Dr. Shirley Guthrie (1927–2004), a Presbyterian minister and Professor of Systematic Theology at Columbia Theological Seminary for nearly 40 years, in his classic *Christian Doctrine*, a standard seminary text, which is also published

---

18. William Temple, Christian Faith and Life (London: Student Christian Movement Press Ltd., 1946), p. 81.
19. Gary Borg, "Church Panel: Take Brimstone from Idea of Hell," *Chicago Tribune*, January 18, 1996.

in Japanese, Korean, Spanish, Taiwanese, and other languages, writes in detail on this topic:

> We have been talking about a point of view which takes death too seriously. Now we have to talk about *false optimism*, which does not take death seriously enough. It is the belief in the immortality of the soul. This doctrine was not taught by the biblical writers themselves, but it was common in the Greek and Oriental religions of the ancient world in which the Christian church was born. Some of the earliest Christian theologians were influenced by it, read the Bible in the light of it and introduced it into the thinking of the church. It has been with us ever since, influencing even the Reformed confessions (see the Westminster Confession, XXXII; the Belgic Confession, Art. XXXVII). According to this doctrine only my body can die, but I myself do not really die. My body is only the shell of my true self. It is not *me*; it is only the earthly-physical prison in which the real 'I' is trapped. My true self is my soul, which, because it is spiritual and not physical, is like God and therefore shares God's immortality (inability to die). What happens at death, then, is that my immortal soul escapes from my mortal body. My body dies, but I myself live on and return to the spiritual realm from which I came and to which I really belong. If we hold to the genuinely biblical hope for the future, we must firmly reject this doctrine of the soul's immortality [....][20]

Guthrie criticizes how the creeds have neatly combined the following:

> [...] the doctrines of the immortality of the soul and the resurrection of the dead. At death, the soul of every man is judged and goes to its eternal destiny, while his body

---

20. Shirley Guthrie, *Christian Doctrine* (Atlanta: George Knox Press, 1968), pp. 381–2, emphasis original.

remains in the grave. On the last day the body is raised again and reunited with the soul for a final judgment (Westminster Confession, XXXIV; Belgic Confession, Art. XXXVII). This theory can be criticized for several reasons: (1) Its separation of body and soul is unbiblical. (2) While it does combine various elements of the biblical hope, the Bible itself does not give us this neat system. The confessions devise an artificial solution to a problem the Bible itself is content to leave unanswered. (3) The final judgment seems completely superfluous if the souls of the righteous and wicked are assigned their permanent places immediately after death. (4) This theory hopelessly confuses the categories of time and eternity. After death a person is beyond our creaturely categories of space and time. Present and future and the time between them (as well as the spatial categories of up and down) are no longer applicable.[21]

- The English word *hell* appears 31 times in the King James version of the Old Testament. In 29 of these instances, the New International Version replaces the KJV *hell* with either the words *grave* or *death*. This is fitting, seeing how the original meaning of the English word *hell* was simply "a covered thing/place."

- The language of destruction that is found throughout the Bible in reference to the wicked is opposed to the popular teaching of eternal conscious torment. Scripture consistently teaches that the fate of the unsaved is to die, to perish, to be destroyed forever—in ways those words are ordinarily understood. (Psalms 37:38, 68:2, 145:20, John 3:16, Philippians 3:19, etc.) If, however, the wicked live forever in unending fire, then they are never destroyed. Also, the biblical imagery of fire (Isaiah 34:10–11, Ezekiel 20:47–48; Amos 5:6, Matthew 3:12, 13:49–50, etc.) suggests obliteration of the wicked, not preservation, since fire consumes what it burns.

---

21. Ibid., p. 396–7.

- The English word *soul* occurs 419 times in the King James version of the Old Testament.[22] In contrast, the New International Version translators used the English word *soul* much more sparingly. When translating the underlying Hebrew word *nephesh* into English, the NIV translators retained the KJV translators' *soul* approximately 25% of the time. Specifically, of the 416 instances where the KJV translators chose to translate the Hebrew *nephesh* with the English word *soul*, the NIV translators chose to do likewise only 110 times.[23] For the remaining 316 occurrences, the NIV translators replaced the KJV's *soul* with a variety of alternative words and phrases, such as: anyone, being, courage, dignity, he, heart, hearted, herself, himself, I, life, me, my, neck, none, one, people, person, self, selves, she, slave, them, thought, us, we, whoever, whole being, you, yourself, and yourselves. This highlights how broad the meaning of the original Hebrew word *nephesh* is and how there is nothing mysteriously sacrosanct or intrinsically special concerning the English word *soul* as found in the Bible. In not one of the instances where *nephesh* appears is there any hint of immortality associated with the term.

- The widely respected *Interpreter's Dictionary of the Bible* says of the soul: "The 'departure' of the *nephesh* [the Hebrew word = 'soul'] must be viewed as a figure of speech, for it does not continue to exist independently of the body, but dies with it (Num. 31:19; Judg. 16:30; Ezek. 13:19). No biblical text authorizes the statement that the 'soul' is separated from the body at the moment of death."[24]

---

22. With only three exceptions (see 2 Samuel 13:39, Psalms 16:2, Job 30:15), the KJV translators chose the word *soul* when translating the Hebrew word *nephesh* into English.

23. There is no textual reason why the NIV translators did replace every occurrence of "soul" with an alternative word. It's possible that because the NIV was translated by a team of scholars rather than by a single individual, it was difficult to be 100% consistent.

24. Edmond Jacob, *The Interpreter's Dictionary of the Bible*, vol. 1, George A. Buttrick, ed. (New York: Abingdon Press, 1962), p. 802.

• The denomination known as the Advent Christian General
  Conference (not affiliated with the Christadelphians) is currently (2022) a member of the National Association of Evangelicals (NAE). What is noteworthy about this denomination
  is that they hold to the very same position regarding the
  death state as the Christadelphians, specifically: "We believe
  that death is a condition of unconsciousness to all persons,
  righteous and wicked; a condition which will remain
  unchanged until the resurrection at Christ's Second Coming,
  at which time the righteous will receive everlasting life while
  the wicked will be 'punished with everlasting destruction'
  suffering complete extinction of being."[25] Should we infer
  from this that the NAE is in association with a cult?[26]

Conclusion

This chapter is not intended to be an exhaustive look at the topic of
conditional immortality and the death state.[27] The facts above are presented to quickly demonstrate that the Christadelphian position cannot
be deemed "strange," nor is it an extreme, novel interpretation with no
possible basis in Scripture or lacking corroboration from Protestant
Christianity. Their views on this topic do not deny any central doctrine
of Christianity. Yes, their position is the minority one historically speaking, but the important point here is that their position does not qualify

---

25. Robert J. Mayer, *Adventism Confronts Modernity* (Eugene: Pickwick, 2017), p. 175.
26. The NAE represents more than 45,000 local churches from 40 different denomina-
    tions and serves a constituency of millions. For a full list of denominations within
    this association, see https://www.nae.org/full-list-of-nae-denominations.
27. There are within Christianity three major views regarding the state of the dead: 1)
    the traditional view where it is believed that all humanity possesses something
    called a "soul," which never dies, and which leaves the body in a state of conscious-
    ness at death to receive its reward either in heaven or in hell (or Purgatory); 2) the
    annihilationist view that denies the existence of anything immortal within man,
    meaning that at death, all life is extinguished; and 3) the hybrid view known as soul-
    sleep, where a belief in an immortal soul is retained but puts that soul into a state of
    unconscious dormancy until the resurrection. Christadelphians hold the annihila-
    tionist view, trusting solely on the resurrection of the dead for any hope of immor-
    tality.

as a characteristic of a cult. If their adversaries wish to label the Christadelphians as a cult and be taken seriously, they will need to find something more substantial to hang their epithet on.

Upon This Rock

And Jesus went forth, and his disciples, into the villages of Caesarea Philippi: and in the way he asked his disciples, saying unto them, Who do men say that I am? And they told him, saying, John the Baptist: and others, Elijah; but others, One of the prophets. And he asked them, But who say ye that I am? Peter answereth and saith unto him, Thou art the Christ.

—MARK 8:27–29, RV

I F THERE IS one doctrinal difference above all others which brings the imprecation of "cult" down upon the heads of the Christadelphians by defenders of mainstream Christianity, it is the position that Christadelphians have taken regarding the identity of God and Jesus. Within the oldest statement of faith compiled by a body of Christadelphians laying out the doctrines forming the basis of their fellowship, these two statements can be found:

- That the only true God is He Who was revealed to Abraham, Isaac and Jacob, by angelic visitation and vision, and to Moses at the flaming bush (unconsumed) and at Sinai, and Who manifested Himself in the Lord Jesus Christ, as the supreme self-existent Deity, the ONE FATHER, dwelling in unapproachable light, yet everywhere present by His Spirit, which is a unity with His person in heaven. He hath, out of His own underived energy, created heaven and earth, and all that in them is.

- That Jesus of Nazareth was the Son of God, begotten of the virgin Mary by the Holy Spirit, without the intervention of man, and afterwards anointed with the same Spirit, without measure, at his baptism.[1]

ɔse unfamiliar with the controversy over the Trinity[2] will not
h to argue with in these words, for it sounds very scriptural at
᠁e value. But what is absent in the Christadelphian statement of faith is
made much plainer in an accompanying section titled "Doctrines to be
Rejected" and which typically accompanies their statements of faith:

[We reject the doctrine of] The Trinity
We believe that God is not three, but One Father, out of whom are
all things—even the Spirit and the Son. (1 Corinthians 8:6; Ephesians 4:6)

**[We reject the doctrine of] The "Eternal Sonship" of Christ, and
the Free-Life Doctrine**
We believe that the Son of God was not co-eternal with the Father,
but is the result of the Father's manifestation in the flesh, by the
operation of the Holy Spirit upon Mary [....] (Luke 1:35; Matthew
1:20; Romans 8:3; Hebrews 2:14,17, 4:15, 5:9; Psalms 21:4)

[We reject the doctrine of] The "Third Person in the Godhead."
We believe that the Holy Spirit is not a person, but the vehicular
effluence of the Father, filling all space, and forming the medium
and instrument of all the Father's operations. (Job 26:13, 33:4;
Psalms 104:30; Nehemiah 9:30)[3]

---

1. Birmingham Statement of Faith. The BASF is the most widely accepted Christadelphian Statement of Faith and comes in two parts. This section is called "Truth to be
   Received," and another section is called "Doctrines to be Rejected." https://en.wiki-
   source.org/wiki/Birmingham_Amended_Statement_of_Faith (accessed October 4,
   2022).
2. The Trinity is more than just a belief in the existence of a triad of three things: Father,
   Son and Spirit of God. Christadelphians believe in the existence of the Father, and in
   the existence of the Son, and the existence of the outworking power or presence of
   God referred to as the Holy Spirit. These are simply three things—a triad. The historical doctrine of the Trinity goes beyond a simple collection of three things. It involves
   a complex and confusing theory which posits that each of these three things are "persons" and that each of the three "persons" are each fully God, each being coeternal
   and coequal with the other "persons," and yet comprising only one God. If this isn't
   confusing enough, by the end of this chapter we'll also discover that "persons" in this
   traditional formula do not actually mean "persons."

This is where the controversy is most obvious. The Christadelphians outright reject the doctrine of the Trinity as defined by 4th century creeds accepted by both Catholics and Protestants. And this is where the mainstream feels especially justified in bringing the charge against the Christadelphians that they are a cult. Orthodoxy asserts that the doctrine of the Trinity is an essential belief of the Christian faith. As strict *sola scriptura* biblicists, however, the Christadelphians would disagree. The remainder of this chapter will be spent examining the historical and Scriptural information that Christadelphians could appeal to in their justification of their non-Trinitarian position.

1: Upon This Rock

When Jesus asked his disciple Simon Peter who he believed Jesus to be, Peter confessed, "You are the Messiah, the Son of the living God" (Matthew 16:16, NLT)—an answer which was drawn from Psalms 2. Jesus highly commended Peter's response, not only by praising its accuracy but also by pronouncing a blessing upon Peter. Jesus stated that this correct understanding of his identity had not been revealed to Peter by men (human learning), but rather Peter had been imparted by divine understanding. "You are blessed, Simon son of John, **because my Father in heaven has revealed this to you**," (v. 17). More importantly, Jesus said Peter's correct recognition of Jesus' identity was to be the "rock" or foundation upon which "I will build my church" (v. 18). Jesus' "church" was not to be built upon a belief (or mystery) that Jesus was something called "God the Son," the "second person" of a Trinity; nor was it to be founded upon a creed that was to be hammered out by one or more ecumenical councils centuries later and which were sometimes convened by emperors and overseen by heads of state. Instead, the Christian faith was to be based upon the belief that Jesus is the Son of God, the Anointed One of God, God's Messiah, as outlined in Psalms 2 and foretold through the words of Moses and the Prophets.

---

3. These are a selection of statements most relevant to the topic under discussion. Minor formatting changes have been made for the sake of this book. For a complete list of rejected doctrines and original formatting, see "Doctrines to be Rejected," *The Christadelphian Advocate*, https://christadelphianadvocate.org/doctrines-to-be-rejected (accessed October 4, 2022).

2: The Son of God

Unlike Peter's confession (above), it is taken for granted among many Christians that to confess Jesus as "the Son of God" is to confess that Jesus is in fact God. It is assumed by them that to affirm that "Jesus is the Son of God" has always meant that Jesus is the preexistent, second "person" of the Trinity, who "for us men and our salvation became incarnate."[4] But this simply does not accord with New Testament evidence. This is not how Peter understood the title, nor any of his fellow apostles. The New Testament never suggests that the title "the Son of God" just means "God."

Based primarily upon Psalms 2 and 2 Samuel 7:12–16, the title "Son of God" was used to refer to a future king of Israel whom God would appoint to rule as a vice-regent over his kingdom on earth. Because the nation of Israel was itself described as a son of God (Exodus 4:22),[5] the promised king who would come to take the nation's destiny on himself could likewise share this title.

Colin Brown (1932–2019), who was senior professor of systematic theology at the conservative and evangelical Fuller Theological Seminary, reminds us:

> [...] the title "Son of God" is not in itself a designation of personal deity or an expression of metaphysical distinctions within the Godhead. Indeed, to be a "Son of God" one has to be a being who is not God! It is a designation for a creature indicating a special relationship with God. In particular, it denotes God's representative, God's vice-regent. It is a designation of kingship, identifying the king as God's son. Therefore, I take the application of the title "Son of God" at his baptism to be an affirmation of Jesus as God's Son-king in virtue of his anointing by the Spirit.
>
> [...] In my view the term "Son of God" ultimately converges on the term "image of God," which is to be understood as

---

4. See the Nicene-Constantinopolitan Creed.
5. The title is not only used of Israel (Exodus 4:22), but also of angels (as in Job 1:6–12), of the king (as in 2 Samuel 7:14), of righteous men (as in Wisdom 2:13–18), or of (other) charismatic rabbis (m. Ta'an. 3:8).

God's representative, the one in whom God's Spirit dwells, and who is given stewardship and authority to act on God's behalf.[6]

Thus, as God's representative on earth, the same homage and obedience due to the principal could be given to the agent, just as if one were in the presence of God himself. Just as a man's son in the father's absence would be assumed to be speaking and acting as his father's agent, so likewise to acknowledge Jesus as the only and beloved "Son of God" would have been to accept him as God's authorized agent, entitled to homage and absolute obedience.

This is how the early Jewish Christians understood this title. They did not think that the title "Son of God" meant that Jesus was some hybrid being, half God and half human, or as the creeds demand, that Jesus was fully God and fully man. It was only with time, as more and more Gentile converts started entering the originally Jewish sect that the original Jewish meaning of the title and the concept of agency began to lose ground.

3: The Greatest Commandment

In Mark 12, Jesus is confronted by the "teachers of the law" (of Moses), who test Jesus by asking him which is the greatest commandment. Jesus responded by quoting the Shema,[7] "Hear, O Israel, the Lord our God, the Lord is one" (Deuteronomy 6:4). His inquisitor quickly approved of Jesus' response, and likewise Jesus commended him back with the words, "You are not far from the kingdom of God."

This is an interesting exchange for the reason that if the Jewish understanding of God's identity was in fact deficient for salvation, here would have been a great time for Jesus to have enlightened his hearers and shared with them a yet unknown but necessary and saving truth. But he did not do so. If belief in the Trinity was to become part of "the greatest commandment," a requirement for salvation, and central to the

---

6. Colin Brown, "Trinity and Incarnation: In Search of a Contemporary Orthodoxy," *Ex Auditu*, vol. 7, 1991, pp. 87–9.

7. The Shema is one of the key prayers of the Jewish ritual, and is a kind of confession of monotheistic faith that devout Israelites are to repeat morning and evening.

Christian faith, then Jesus could have done a much better job than he did here. Why did he not answer with something like this?: "It is written in your Law that the Lord our God, the Lord is one; but I say unto you, I am the Lord your God! I am one of three, and we be three in one. Hear O Israel if ye have ears to hear!" Instead, Jesus left the "teachers of the law" with the same understanding of God that they came to him with. If the doctrine of the Trinity is true, why did Jesus leave the greatest commandment unchanged and the bedrock of Judaism firmly in place?

4: The Father, the only true God = Eternal Life

In John 17:1-3, Jesus says, "Father...this is eternal life, that they might know thee **the only true God**, and Jesus Christ whom thou have sent."[8] If the Father is "the only true God," then what are we to make of the Trinitarian claim that Jesus is also "God"? Are there more than one "only true Gods"?

5: The Uncapitalized "word"

The first seven English translations of the Bible, starting with John Wycliffe's translation of 1380, and including William Tyndale's translation (1526-1536, see next page), all used a lowercase rendering of the word "word" (or "worde") in the prologue of John's Gospel. It wasn't until the first committee-translated Bible was published—The Geneva Bible in 1560—that an English reader would have discovered a capitalized "Word" referring to the Greek *logos* in the opening verses of John chapter 1. This is important because of how the average reader today interprets a capitalized word versus an uncapitalized word. In modern English, personalized names are capitalized, therefore capitalizing the word *Word* can suggest to the reader that this regular noun should be read as a proper name. Capitalizing the word associated with the Greek *logos*, a word that occurs twenty-five times in the gospels (and never there capitalized outside of John 1), can easily mislead a reader.

---

8. Emphasis added.

⟨ The Gofpell of Saynct
Jhon the Apoſtle and Euangeliſt.

⟨ Jhon Baptiſt bare wytnes of Chriſt.
The Iewes eucupyed of S. John yf he were Chriſt.
Of the callynge of Andrew/Peter/Philip/and Nathanael.

⟨ The fyrſt Chapter. ✠

A the begyn=
nyng was the
woorde / and
ÿ woorde was
with God: and the word
was god. The fame was
in the begynnynge with
God. All thynges were
made by it/ꝫ without it/
was made nothyng that
was made. Jn it was ly=
fe/ and the lyfpe was the
lyght of men/ꝫ the lyght
fhyneth in the darcknes/
but the darcknes compre
hended it not.

There was a man fent
frome God/ whofe name
was John. The fame came as a witnes/ to beare witnes of the
lyght/ that all mē through him myght beleue. He was not that
lyghte / but to beare wytnes of the lyghte. That was a true
lyght whiche lyghteth all men that come into the woorlde. He
was in the woorlde/ and the woorlde was made by him : and yet
the woorlde knewe him not.

He came among his owne/ and his owne receaued him not.
But as many as receaued hym / to them he gaue power to be
the fones of God/ in that they beleued on his name: which were
borne not of bloude/ nor of the wyll of the flefhe/ nor yet of the
wyll of man: but of God.

And the worde was made flefhe and dwelt amonge vs/ and Math. i.c
we fawe the glory of it / as the glory of the onlye begotten fone Luce. 4.d
of the father/ which worde was full of grace and verite. ▐
  ✠ John

Above: William Tyndale's English translation of the Gospel of John, chapter 1 (1536). Tyndale chose to translate the pronoun associated with the Greek word λογος (English: "word") as "it" rather than "he." This practice continued in subsequent English translations of John, including Matthews' (1537), Cranmer's (1539), Taverner's (1540), and Whittingham's first Geneva Bible (1557). Observe also that Tyndale rendered "word" in lowercase letters, as did Matthews, Cranmer, Taverner and Whittingham (1557).

THE HOLY

GOSPEL OF IESVS

CHRISTE, VVRIT

by sainct Iohn.

***

THE FYRST CHAPTER.

The diuinitie, humanitie, and office of Ie-
sus Christe. The testimonie of Iohn. The callyng
of Andrewe, Peter, &c.

A
" N THE begin- " Or, before
nyng was the the begyn-
word, & ẏ worde ning.
" was with God, "Christ is God
& ᵃthat worde was "Before all ty
God. me.
2 The same was *Col. 1. b.*
" in the begyn- " No creatu-
nyng ẇ God. re was made
without
Christ.

ᵃ The Sonne is
of the same subsã
ce with the Father.

3 * Althinges were made by it, & " without " Wherby all
it was made nothing that was made. thinges are
quickened &
4 In it was " lyfe, and the lyfe was the preserued.
ᵇ light of men. "Mans mynde
is ful of dar-
5 And the light shineth in " darkenes, & kenes, becau-
the darknes comprehended it not. se of the cor-
ruptiõ therof.
Rom. 1. c.

ᵇ The life of mã
is more excellent
then of any other
creature: because
it is ioyned with
light & vnderstan-
ding.

6 * There

Above: William Whittingham's English translation of John, chapter 1 (1557). Whitting-ham chose to translate the pronoun associated with the Greek word λογος (English: "word") as "it" rather than "he," as did his English predecessors, Tyndale (1526-1536), Matthews (1537), Cranmer (1539), and Taverner (1540). He, like Tyndale, also rendered the word "word" in lowercase letters. If a mainstream Protestant translator of the Bible were to do likewise today, there would be a public outcry among Evangelicals and defenders of the Trinity and possible calls for banning the translation for use in

Here is how the text was translated in the 14th century, in the first complete English translation ever published: "In the bigynnyng was the word, and the word was at God, and God was the word," (John Wycliffe, *The New Testament*, 1380).

With respect to its meaning, *logos* means *an idea* or *the thoughts expressed in words*. Nowhere in the four gospels is this *logos* identified as a person. It was God's *logos*, that is, His active word, or plan and purpose that was made manifest in the birth and life of Jesus. It is in this sense that the word (*logos*) was made flesh (John 1:14).

6: A Neutered "word"

Another important truth concerning John's Prologue can be discovered through a similar examination of the earliest of the English translations. Tyndale's translation of John 1 (see two pages over), along with Matthews' (1537), Cranmer's (1539) (which was the first Bible authorized by the Church of England), Taverner's (1540), and Whittingham's (1557)—all of these early English Bible translations used the neuter pronoun *it* in John 1:1–3 to describe "the word" (*logos*) of John 1:1. An example:

> In the begynnynge was the worde, and the worde was wyth God; and God was the worde. The same was in the begynnyng wyth God. All thinges were made by **it**, and wythout **it**, was made nothynge that was made. In **it** was lyfe, and the lyfe was the lyght of men, and the lyght shyneth in darcknes, and the darcknes comprehended **it** not. (The Great Bible/Cranmer's, 1539)

Today, however, it would be impossible to find a commercialized English translation of the New Testament that hasn't succumbed to what is an obvious *translation bias*. Today, almost universally, the original "it" has been replaced with a capitalized "He," which unquestionably colors the text with a Trinitarian hue and greatly alters how the Prologue might otherwise be understood. If all things were made through "the word" as an *it*, a quite different meaning of the Prologue emerges: the "word" in John 1 could not be viewed as a second "person" existing alongside God the Father from "the beginning." Consequently, one of the main planks and proof-texts of Trinitarianism (and Arianism) would be removed.

7: Getting the Cart in Front of the Horse

This next point also pertains to the prologue to John's Gospel and can be best summarized by Colin Brown, senior professor of systematic theology at Fuller Theological Seminary:

> It is a common but patent misreading of the opening of John's Gospel to read it as if it said: "In the beginning was the *Son*, and the *Son* was with God, and the *Son* was God." (John 1:1). What has happened here is the substitution of *Son* for *Word* (Greek *logos*), and thereby the *Son* is made a member of the Godhead which existed from the beginning. But if we follow carefully the thought of John's Prologue, it is the *Word* that preexisted eternally with God and is God. The same Word that made all things [....][9]

Moreover, if by the term "God" in John 1:1 Trinitarians understand it to refer to the first person of the Trinity, and by the term "Word" they understand it to refer to the second person of the Trinity, then there exists a problem. Read the verse according such an interpretation: "In the beginning was the second person of the Trinity, and the second person was with the first person of the Trinity, and the second person was the first person in the Trinity." This is the necessary and inevitable consequence to which the Trinitarian interpretation leads.

8: Where is the Accusation?

When Jesus was brought before the chief priest after his arrest, witnesses were brought forth to accuse Jesus of crimes that they hoped would be worthy of his death. Of all of the accusations brought against

---

9. Colin Brown, "Trinity and Incarnation: In Search of a Contemporary Orthodoxy," *Ex Auditu*, v. 7, 1991, p. 89.

him, not one person charged Jesus with the crime that he had claimed to be God. If, in fact, Jesus claimed to be God, as Trinitarians believe him to be, and his teachings on this "truth" were undermining the faith of the Jewish people, then why was such a charge not brought against him at his trial? When the religious authorities were eager to seize on the most trifling circumstance, when they sought long for two witnesses that would agree, is it possible they would pass by such a charge as this—that Jesus claimed to be God? And since they were entirely silent concerning this "truth," is it not certain that he could never have made any such claim? A man who believed himself to be God Almighty—the God of Israel, Yahweh walking around in the flesh—this would have been more problematic to and more worthy of condemnation by the Jewish religious authorities than the charge that was ultimately brought against Jesus, which was that he said he was "the Son of God," a kingly title which signified a potential political threat to the Romans, and for which he was ultimately doomed to death.

9: Sent by God

Being "sent by God" does not prove that the individual being sent preexisted in heaven before being commissioned. Joseph (Genesis 45:5), Moses (Exodus 3:10, 5:22, 7:16), unnamed prophets (Judges 6:8, 2 Kings 17:13, 2 Chronicles 25:15, Jeremiah 25:4), the judges Jerubbaal, Bedan, Jephthah, and Samuel (1 Samuel 12:11), a bed-ridden and immobile Ahijah (1 Kings 14:6), Elijah (2 Kings 2:2), Jeremiah (Jer. 26:12), Zechariah (Zech. 4:9), and John the Baptist (Matthew 11:10, Mark 1:2, John 1:6) were all described as being "sent by God," yet are we to suppose that these individuals all preexisted in heaven when God "sent" them to do His will on earth? No.

To find Jesus described in the Bible as one who was "sent by God" (Matthew 10:40, Mark 9:37, Luke 4:18,43, 9:48, etc.) is in keeping with the language of *agency* that was common within Hebrew and ancient culture. Similarly, a statement that something has come "from heaven" doesn't prove that it preexisted in heaven. Did Nicodemus the Pharisee think that Jesus had a preexistence in heaven when he said to Jesus, "We know that you are a teacher *come from God*" (John 3:2)? John the Baptist's "ministry of baptizing" is described as having originated "from heaven" (Matthew 21:25, Mark 11:30, Luke 20:4). So too was the miraculous manna from heaven despite the fact that it simply appeared each day on the ground like dew (Exodus 16:4–13, Nehemiah 9:15, Psalms 105:40). This ground-based "manna from heaven" is what Jesus was comparing himself to when he described himself as the "living bread...from heaven" in John 6:35–38.

10: Worshiping Jesus

It is argued by Trinitarians that one proof that Jesus must be God is found in the fact that Jesus received worship while upon earth. Trinitarians claim that the many acts of homage and petition paid to Jesus should have been rejected by him upon a principle of piety if he was merely a created being. Such honors were of too high a nature to be paid to any one unless he was invested with true and full "divinity." The Trinitarian argument goes something like this: "God alone is the legitimate recipient of worship. He forbids directing worship to any other being or object in Heaven or on earth." They then assert, "God makes it abundantly clear that His Son, the Messiah, is entitled to receive worship, and He [the Son] therefore is God."[10]

But do the Scriptures really represent Jesus as the proper object for prayer and spiritual worship? First, consider how Jesus not only taught others, but himself prayed to his Father only, as is apparent from numerous passages in the New Testament, and he expressly desired that religious homage might be paid to his Father only: "Glorify **your Father** who is in heaven." "Pray to **your Father** who is in secret." "Pray then like this: **Our Father** who art in heaven." "The hour is coming when you shall neither in this mountain nor at Jerusalem worship **the Father**. [...] The time is coming and now is, when the true worshippers shall worship **the Father** in spirit and in truth." "If you ask anything of **the Father**, he will give it to you."[11]

Part of the flaw in the Trinitarian argument is simply that the English word "worship" has a wide range of meaning. For example, in

---

10. Stanley Rosenthal, *The Tri-Unity of God in the Old Testament* (Bellmawr: The Friends of Israel Gospel Ministry, Inc., 1978), p. 10.
11. Matthew 5:10, 6:6, Luke 11:2, John 4:21–23, John 15:16.

the British legal system, judges have regularly been addressed as "Your Worship," but in doing so, no one who uses this form of address thinks that these judges are the God of the universe. In the Anglican Church, the *Book of Common Prayer* contains the format for the marriage service, which include the words, "With my body I thee worship." Yet, no one believes that the Anglican Church is promoting idolatry with the use of such language.

In the New Testament, the word often translated into English as *worship* originates from the Greek *proskyneō*. A quick look at this word's usage in the NT reveals that its meaning is not restricted to the exclusive worship of God. For example, in Revelation 3:9 Jesus says to the Christians at the church of Philadelphia that they would shortly be "worshiped" by one of their adversaries:

> Behold, I will make them of the synagogue of Satan, which say they are Jews, and are not, but do lie; behold, I will make them to come and worship before thy feet, and to know that I have loved thee. (KJV)

And in Matthew 18:26, the Parable of the Unforgiving Servant has the first servant "worshiping" [*proskynein*] before the king to whom he owes a great sum of money:

> The servant therefore fell down, and worshipped him, saying, Lord, have patience with me, and I will pay thee all. (KJV)

In the Ancient Near East, this type of "worship" was commonly paid to kings and other superiors, both by Jews and non-Jews. An interesting example of the use of this Greek word is found in the Septuagint version of 1 Chronicles 29:20. Here *proskynein* (KJV, RV, ASV: "worship") is offered *both* to God *and* to King David: "And all the congregation blessed the LORD, the God of their fathers, and bowed down their heads, and worshipped the LORD, and the king," (RV). The "worship" of the king could coexist with the "worship" of God without contradiction, for the king had been appointed and anointed by God as His vice-regent, and served as an agent/broker on behalf of God in the rule and judgment of the people of God (Israel).

Jerome H. Neyrey, a Jesuit priest and Professor of New Testament
Studies at the University of Notre Dame, says of this term:

> When examined critically, "worship" [*proskyneō*] basically
> describes the showing of respect to someone, respect depending
> on the role and status of the one approached. Mortals indeed
> honored Jesus, bowing down before him, even addressing him
> with special names and titles, but they honored Jesus of Naza-
> reth in terms of his broker relationship to God. Petitioners acted
> appropriately to solicit their patron or broker to act on their
> behalf. Respect and honor, but not worship. [...] All depends on
> the role and status of the person shown respect; respect shown
> brokers and mediators should never be confused with that
> shown a Patron.
>
> Lack of awareness of the patron-broker-client model of com-
> mon social relationships results in failure to appreciate the dif-
> ferent roles which these three actors play, and the proper
> etiquette with which each should be approached.[12]

J. L. North, a Senior Lecturer in New Testament Studies at Hull University, adds:

> προσκύνησις [*proskynesis*, English: "worshiping"] suggests a
> variety of physical postures adopted for any one of several rea-
> sons and directed to any number of possible recipients. It con-
> notes homage, respect, honour, reverence. It can be offered to
> God or human beings or even the inanimate. The implication
> for the early church is that it cannot mean 'worship' in any sense
> that compels us to infer the deity of Christ.[13]

In contrast to *proskyneō*, the Greek verb *latreuō* is used twenty-one
times in the New Testament, and always in the sense of cultic or religious service, but never once is it used in reference to Jesus.[14]

---

12. Jerome H. Neyrey, "Was Jesus of Nazareth a Monotheist?," *Biblical Theology Bulletin*,
vol. 49, no. 3 (2019), pp. 142–3.
13. J. Lionel North, "Jesus and Worship, God and Sacrifice," *Early Jewish and Christian
Monotheism*, Loren T. Stuckenbruck, ed. (London: T & T Clark, 2004), p. 195.

One must therefore conclude that the Trinitarian assertion that Jesus must be God because he received "worship" is simply untrue. New Testament scholar, professor and Anglican cleric, Richard T. France, concisely summarizes:

> [...] the gospels do not provide clear evidence that Jesus was worshipped in the formal sense during His lifetime. That requests were addressed to Him, including requests for miraculous help (e.g. Mk. 1:40; 5:22f.; Mt. 8:25; 14:30) is not evidence of worship, any more than it would be in the case of any one else who was known to heal by the power of God. Nor need the fact that many such requests include the address *kyrie* ('Lord') imply divine honours, despite the clearly divine implications of that title as used later, for *kyrie* as addressed to a living person was a polite form appropriate to anyone regarded as in some sense superior to the speaker, more deferential than our 'Sir', but far from implying divinity. Similarly, the mention that suppliants and others 'worshipped' Him, as the AV put it (e.g. Mk. 5:6; Mt. 8:2; 9:18), or knelt before Him (e.g. Mk. 10:17; Mt. 17:14), while it clearly conveyed more than mere politeness particularly to Matthew, who is fond of the verb *proskynein*, does not in the historical context of Jesus' ministry necessarily imply what 'worship' means to us; it is more than social politeness, but is not a gesture appropriate only to God (see e.g. Mt. 18:26; Rev. 3:9).[15]

11: Agency

This next point is related to the previous one and may qualify as one of the two best kept secrets within Christianity, which when understood, greatly helps clear up the confusion that sometimes occurs regarding Jesus' relationship to God. This little known fact affected how Jesus spoke and acted, and how others could speak of him as being

---

14. Both words occur in Matthew 4:10, "...for it is written, 'You shall worship [*proskunesis*] the Lord your God and him only shall you serve [*latreusis*].'" (RSV)
15. Richard T. France, "The Worship of Jesus—A Neglected Factor In Christological Debate?," *Vox Evangelica*, vol. 12 (1981), pp. 25-6.

"equal to God" without any risk of misunderstanding who Jesus actually was. I am referring to the concept of *agency*. The principle of Jewish agency is that "an agent is like the one who sent him."[16] A. E. Harvey, Anglican minister and Canon Theologian at Westminster Abbey, provides more insight behind Jewish agency when he writes:

> As soon as an agent's credentials were authenticated, he became (so far as the transaction in hand was concerned) 'like' the principal himself: it was *as if* the principal was present. So with God's agent: as soon as one was convinced that he was really authorized by God, it was *as if* God was present—and there could be no limit to the transactions which the agent might undertake on God's behalf; he would certainly be involved in those which were specifically associated with God, such as forgiving, healing, and judging.[17]

Jesus is presented in the Gospels against the backdrop of the Jewish concept of agency. Agency goes a long way toward explaining the following features of Johannine Christology in particular: the unity of the work of the Father and Son; seeing God through the Son; the call to honor the Son as one would honor God; and the language of sending.

12: Jewish Preexistence

Perhaps the second best kept secret pertaining to the biblical description of Jesus and his identity relates to how the Jewish authors of the New Testament books, and Jesus himself, used the language of "preexistence" to describe things which were foreordained (predetermined) by God from before Creation or at the moment of Creation.

Jewish authors and sages had a very specific way of emphasizing the great importance they attached to certain central values in Jewish religious life and thought: they made statements to the effect that the features in question were "preexistent" in the sense that they were either

---

16. Peder Borgen, *The Gospel of John: More Light from Philo, Paul and Archaeology* (Leiden: Koninklijke Brill, 2014), p. 14.

17. Anthony Ernest Harvey, "Christ as Agent," *The Glory of Christ in the New Testament*, L. D. Hurst and N. T. Wright, eds. (Oxford: Clarendon Press, 1987), p. 247.

actually created in the six days of Genesis or their idea came up in God's mind at that seminal time. Among the things mentioned as ideally pre-existing were the Torah, Repentance, the Garden of Eden (Paradise) and Gehenna, God's Throne of Glory, the Fathers (Abraham, Isaac and Jacob), Israel, the Temple—and the Messiah.[18] The concept of the preexistence of the Messiah accords with the general Talmudic view which holds that "The Holy One, blessed be He, prepares the remedy before the wound" (*Babylonian Talmud*, Meg. 13b).[19] In other words, there was a general belief among the Jews that the appearance of the Messiah was part of the Creator's plan from the inception of the universe. In the mind of God, things of utmost importance in His plan with his Creation can—and do—exist with such a degree of reality that they can be said to have "real" existence, or "preexistence." This is why both Moses and Jacob can be found as preexisting their births in ancient Jewish writings.[20] This is why the kingdom of God is described as having been prepared "from the foundation of the world" (Matthew 25:34), and how the righteous had been chosen before the foundation of the world (Ephesians 1:4), with their names having been written in the book of life from the foundation of the world (Revelation 13:8, 17:8).

Failing to understand this uniquely Jewish way of thinking and speaking accounts for much of mainstream Christianity's confusion with regard to Jesus' identity and his nature. Unlike Trinitarians and Arians (such as the Jehovah's Witnesses), Christadelphians hold to the Jewish view of ideal preexistence as it pertains to the identity of the Messiah. In other words, Christadelphians do not believe that Jesus literally preexisted his birth, but rather that the Messiah was in the mind and plan of God from the very inception of the universe, who God foreordained to redeem His creation. As the apostle Peter explains, "Christ, who was foreknown indeed before the foundation of the world, but was manifested at the end of the times for your sake" (1 Peter 1:19-20).

---

18. Raphael Patai, *The Messiah Texts* (Detroit: Wayne State Univ. Press, 1979), pp. 16-7. Examples of ideal preexistence can also be found in the New Testament, most commonly found in conjunction with the phrase "before the foundation of the world." See Matthew 25:34, Acts 15:18, Romans 4:17, 1 Corinthians 2:7, Ephesians 1:4, 2 Timothy 1:9, Titus 1:1-2, 1 Peter 1:19-20, Revelation 13:8, 17:8.

19. Ibid., pp. 16-7.

20. See for example, The *Assumption of Moses*, 1.14: "Moses says, 'He designed and devised me, and he prepared me before the foundation of the world that I should be the mediator of his covenant.'"

As previously noted, this concept of the ideal preexistence of the Messiah accords with the general Talmudic view which teaches that God prepares the cure before the wound. Thus, the role and purpose of Sonship preexisted, but the Son of God himself, did not.

13: Unity Does Not Imply Ontological Equality

One of the most common "go to" proof-texts utilized by Trinitarians is from John 10:30, where Jesus states, "I and my Father are one." But the unity expressed in this verse was not one of essence or substance, but of purpose. There are many ways in which two or more persons can be said to be one without experiencing unity in an ontological sense. One example is marriage, where a man and a woman become "one flesh" (Genesis 2:24). Another example can be found in John 17:11, where Jesus prayed for oneness among his disciples "as we are one," that is, just as the Father and Son are "one." Yet just as the unity among the followers of Jesus was not a unity of essence, but rather of purpose, so was the oneness Jesus spoke of between himself and the Father in John 10:30. Moreover, since 10:29 unequivocally states that "my Father is greater than all," which Jesus repeats in John 14:28, there should be no occasion for Trinitarians to claim that some divine nature can be found in these texts. And yet many have claimed such, and still do.

Going as far back as the second century, early Church fathers, with the exception of Origen, took John 10:30 as teaching the ontological equality between the Father and the Son.[21] Yet during the Reformation period, both Philip Melanchthon and John Calvin, who were staunch defenders of the Trinity, questioned whether this text could be appropriated as a proof of the deity of Jesus. These Protestant reformers understood the "oneness" spoken of in John 10:30 as a oneness of purpose and will. Calvin went so far to as harshly criticize the Church fathers for their exegetical overreach, stating: "The ancients made a wrong use of this passage to prove that Christ is *homoousios*, of the same essence with the Father. For Christ does not argue about the unity of substance [in

---

21. T. E. Pollard, "The Exegesis of John X. 30 in the Early Trinitarian Controversies," *New Testament Studies*, vol. 3, no. 4 (July 1957), pp. 334–49.

the Godhead] but about the agreement which he has with the Father
[....]"[22]

14: My Lord and My Elohim

It sounds like stating something obvious, but Jesus' disciple
Thomas was not an Englishman. This being the case, Thomas undoubt-
edly did not speak the English words that we find in John 20:28, "My
Lord and my God." Remember, what we have in our English Bibles is a
translation from the Greek text.

Thomas was a Jew, not a Greek. It is improbable that a Jew would
speak Greek to another Jew (in this case: Jesus), especially in Jerusalem
in the first century. Instead, Thomas would have spoken Aramaic or
Hebrew in his conversations with Jesus. Therefore, the two Hebrew
words that Thomas likely used in response to encountering the risen
Jesus in this context would have been *adohnee* and *elohim*. Thomas most
likely expressed himself this way: "My *adohnee* and my *elohim*."

Adohnee is a word and title given to anyone who has a higher rank
than themselves. It is commonly translated as "lord," a term that servants would use to address their masters (Matthew 24:48), and even
wives used with respect to their husbands (1 Peter 3:6). The second
word, *elohim*, although it can be translated as "God" in English, is better
understood as "one who possesses powers"—*powers* in the sense implied
within the expression "the powers that be." *Elohim* could be used to
denote individuals who had authority to judge: e.g., kings, judges,
angels, and yes, of course, the God of Israel.[23]

This is exactly what we find in the Old Testament, for the word *elohim* has there been applied to God's angels, to Moses and to the rulers of
Israel, in addition to Yahweh Himself. Therefore, it would not have been
blasphemous for a Jew to have used the term *elohim* with respect to a
man such as Jesus, for as Jesus himself pointed out to the Pharisees in
John 10:34–36, men in the scriptures are sometimes called "gods"

---

22. John Calvin, *Reformation Commentary on Scripture*, NT IV, John 1–12, Craig S.
Farmer, ed. (Downers Grove: InterVarsity Press, 2014), p. 396.
23. *Biblical Commentary on the Epistle to the Hebrews*, John Fulton, transl. (Edinburgh:
T. & T. Clark, 1853), p. 52.

(*elohim*)—men to whom the word of God had come and who were channels of God's communication.

Another way to understand Thomas' confession is to view him as addressing the Father (God) indirectly through Jesus. Jesus had, after all, previously stated that, "He who sees me sees him who sent me ... For I have not spoken on my own authority; the Father who sent me has himself given me commandment what to say and what to speak" (John 12:45-49, RSV), and throughout John's narrative both John and Jesus made it clear that Jesus was an agent of God.

Lastly, this description "Lord (sovereign/king) and God" is nearly identical to Philo's elevated description of Moses in his *Life of Moses*. Philo (c. 20 B.C. – c. 50 A.D.) was a Hellenistic-Jewish philosopher who lived in Alexandria, Egypt. His goal was the intellectual accommodation of Jewish to Greek thought similar in many ways to what we see in the patristic period when early church "fathers" sought to harmonize Greek philosophy with Christian teaching. Philo reports in 1:158 that Moses had been given the very same divine title that Thomas used in the presence of Jesus. Philo, speaking concerning Moses, states: "Again, was not the joy of his partnership with the Father and Maker of all magnified also by the honor of being deemed worthy to bear the same title? For he was named god and king of the whole nation...."

Philo most certainly did not believe that Moses was Yahweh, the Almighty God of heaven and earth, though he bestowed the lofty title of "God and king" upon Moses. It is very possible—indeed most logical given Thomas' Jewish beliefs—that Thomas proclaimed in the presence of Jesus nothing more than what Philo did when referring to Moses with the same terms.

Thomas' words to Jesus in John 20:8, therefore, can easily be understood as an example of *Jewish agency*, where the risen Jesus stood once more as an agent of God. There was no confusion in the mind of Thomas. Thomas was not confusing or conflating the Son of God with God. As German Protestant pastor and professor of theology, Johannes Heinrich August Ebrard (1818–1888) reminds us:

> It was not foreign to the Israelitish mode of conception and expression, to denote persons who stood as the agents and representatives of God by the word אלהים [elohim/god] (sing.) [...] They were thus denoted, not because they were

regarded as creatures equal with God, but because, in their relation to those who were subject to them, they were clothed with divine authority.[24]

15: My God, My God, My God, My God!

John 20:28 is not the only place where we can find the words "my God" and Jesus in close proximity to one other.[25] For example, when Jesus was hanging on the cross: "about the ninth hour Jesus cried with a loud voice, 'Eli, Eli, lama sabachthani?' that is, 'My God, my God, why hast thou forsaken me?'" (Matthew 27:46, RSV). In addition to revealing the deep agony and sense of despair experienced by Jesus in his final hours, his words "my God, my God" confirm an easy to overlook truth: Jesus had a God.

This simple truth—that there was a God over him whom he worshiped and served, and whom he referred to in John 17:3 as "the only true God"—this truth was reaffirmed by Jesus after his resurrection. Prior to ascending to this God, Jesus stated, "Go to my brethren and say to them, I am ascending to my Father and your Father, to my God and your God" (John 20:17, RSV).[26]

This very same reference to "my God" (i.e., the God of Jesus) can be found upon Jesus' lips even *after* he ascended into heaven, and even *after* he was "exalted at the right hand of God" (Acts 2:33). In Revelation 3:12, the exalted Son for a total of four times uses these very same words, "my God," to affirm that he *still* has a God over him:

He who conquers, I will make him a pillar in the temple of **my God**; never shall he go out of it, and I will write on him the

---

24. Johannes Heinrich August Ebrard, *Biblical Commentary on the Epistle to the Hebrews*, John Fulton, transl. (Edinburgh: T. & T. Clark, 1853), p. 52.

25. A noteworthy variant where the two ideas are found together is Psalm 89:20–27, "I have found David, my servant; with my holy oil I have anointed him [....] He shall cry to me, 'Thou art my Father, my God, and the Rock of my salvation.'" A strong case can be made that the "David" being referred to in this passage has a dual application, first to the patriarch David, Israel's anointed king, but ultimately to the greater son of David, the Messiah Jesus. In this second application, the prophet who is speaking of things to come, proclaims that he (the Messiah, though not yet born) has a God over him: "...my Father, my God...."

name of **my God**, and the name of the city of **my God**, the new
Jerusalem which comes down from **my God** out of heaven,
and my own new name. (Revelation 3:12, RSV)[27]

16: Scratch That

The once-popular text found in 1 John 5:7, which for centuries had
been used to support the doctrine of the Trinity, has been proven by
scholars to be a 4th century forgery. "For there are three that bear record
in heaven, the Father, the Word, and the Holy Ghost: and these three are
one," did not exist in the original Greek text, for if it had, it would have
most surely been employed by one of the Greek Fathers in the Trinitarian controversies of their time.[28] Yet none of them did. The phrasing
"three that bear record... these three are one" is found in no Greek man-
uscript earlier than the fourteenth century. Systematic theologian,
Charles C. Ryrie, whose commentary notes can be found in nearly 3
million study Bibles, says of this passage:

> [...] the New Testament contains no explicit statement of the
> doctrine of the triunity of God (since "these three are one" in 1
> John 5:7 is apparently not a part of the genuine text of scripture)
> [....][29]

---

26. This statement by Jesus raises some uncomfortable yet necessary questions for Trin-
    itarians: If God is a Trinity, consisting of three coequal "persons," then why is it that
    Jesus always identifies the Father with this one God? Why does Jesus never refer to
    the Holy Spirit as God? Was Jesus here ascending to only one of the three "persons"
    in the "Godhead"? Why didn't Jesus say, "I am ascending to my Father, and your
    Father, and to the Holy Spirit...?" Why is it that the Holy Spirit is always absent in NT
    passages where Jesus interacts with and refers to God, e.g., when Jesus prays to the
    Father? Why does Jesus never pray to the Holy Spirit? Why are worshipers exhorted
    to worship the Father at the exclusion of the remaining coequal "persons" of the
    "Godhead" (John 4:23)? Why are we instructed to pray to the Father alone, if all
    three "persons" of the Trinity are coequal (Matthew 6:9, Luke 11:12)?
27. Emphasis added.
28. Adam Clarke, *The New Testament of Our Lord and Saviour Jesus Christ*, vol. 2 (New
    York: A. Paul, 1823), p. 856.
29. Charles C. Ryrie, *Basic Theology* (Chicago: Moody Publishers, 1999), p. 60.

Even Martin Luther excluded the disputed text when translating his German Bible. Unfortunately, his English counterparts had fewer scruples. The disputed text has been included in nearly every English translation published from the middle of the 16th century through the 19th century. Today, however, no modern Bible translation includes the verse with the exception of the New King James.

Yet it should not be forgotten, as the classical scholar Lewis Campbell reminds us, that "for two centuries and more, no clergyman could have questioned the authority of this verse, without incurring the danger of being reputed a Socinian [Unitarian heretic]."[30]

17: Baptizing in the Name of ...?

Now that most Trinitarian defenders have abandoned 1 John 5:7 as a proof-text, Matthew 28:19 has become the strongest and most commonly cited passage used in support of the doctrine of the Trinity:

> Go therefore and make disciples of all nations, baptizing them in the name of the Father and of the Son and of the Holy Spirit. (RSV)

This verse is the only place where the three terms "Father," "Son," and "Holy Spirit" are found together in all of the New Testament, which is why this passage is so commonly employed as a proof-text by Trinitarians. However, as the Unitarian Henry Ware bluntly points out:

> Does it say that they are three persons? No, it does not say that they are persons at all.—Does it assert that they constitute one God? No. Does it say that each is God? No such thing. Does it say that they are all equal? No such thing. Does it say they are all to be worshipped? No. Then it does not teach the doctrine of the Trinity. If it neither declares them to be three persons, nor equal to each other, nor each to be God, nor each to be worshipped, then it does not teach the doctrine of the Trinity.[31]

---

30. Lewis Campbell, "On the Revision of the English New Testament," C(
   Review, vol. 28 (August 1867) (London: Henry S. King and Co., 1876), p.

What we have in Matthew 28:19 is not the Trinity, but a triad—a triad of three things—such as we find in 1 Corinthians 10:2 when Paul says, "Our fathers were baptized into Moses, in the cloud, and in the sea." Does this triad prove that Moses was divine and that he, the cloud, and the sea are all coequal and coeternal? Must we conclude that the Father, Son, and the holy angels at Luke 9:26 are one essence or single being because we find there a "glorified" association of three "divine" things?[32] No.

Some Protestant scholars can see the problem that Ware and I are trying to highlight:

> This text [Matthew 28:19], however, taken by itself, would not prove decisively either the *personality* of the three subjects mentioned, or their *equality* or *divinity*. For (a) the subject into which one is baptized is not necessarily a *person*, but may be a *doctrine* or *religion*. (b) The person in whom one is baptized is not necessarily God, as 1Co 1:13, 'Were ye baptized in the name of Paul?' (c) The connection of these three subjects does not prove their *personality* or *equality*.[33]

This is not the only flaw with the Trinitarian argument. A greater concern is that there are serious reasons to doubt whether the command to baptize into the three-fold name was even given by Jesus in the first place.

German Jesuit priest and theologian Karl Rahner expressed his concern regarding the authenticity of the passage when he wrote: "it must be noted that modern exegesis does not count this saying among the *ipsissima verba* [actual words] of Jesus."[34] German Lutheran theologian

---

31. Henry Ware, Jr., *Outline of the Testimony of Scripture Against the Trinity* (Boston: American Unitarian Assoc., 1832), pp. 5–6.

32. "For whoever is ashamed of me and of my words, of him will the Son of man be ashamed when he comes in his glory and the glory of the Father and of the holy angels." (RSV)

33. "Trinity," *Cyclopaedia of Biblical, Theological, and Ecclesiastical Literature*, vol. 10, John McClintock and James Strong, eds. (New York: Harper and Bros., 1886), p. 552. Strong (1822–1894) was an American academic, biblical scholar, lexicographer, Methodist theologian and professor, best known for being the creator of *Strong's Concordance*.

and prominent Church historian Adolf von Harnack echoed the sentiment:

> [...] Matt. XXVIII. 19, is not a saying of the Lord. The reasons for this assertion are. (i) It is only a later stage of the tradition that represents the risen Christ as delivering speeches and giving commandments. Paul knows nothing of it. (2) The Trinitarian formula is foreign to the mouth of Jesus and has not the authority in the Apostolic age which it must have had, if it had descended from Jesus himself.[35]

The authenticity of Matthew 28:19 has been challenged on historical as well as on textual and literary grounds. From the historical perspective,

> It must be acknowledged that the formula of the threefold name, which is here enjoined, does not appear to have been employed by the primitive Church, which, so far as our information goes, baptised 'in' or 'into the name of Jesus' (or 'Jesus Christ' or 'the Lord Jesus': Ac 238 816 1048 195; cf. 1 Co 113, 15), without reference to the Father or the Spirit.[36]

In the book of Acts there are eight baptismal accounts, each one of which gives us a window into how the apostles understood the words of Jesus in Matthew 28:19. If Jesus had indeed introduced a triune formula, one would certainly expect to find the apostles repeating it as they went out into the nations making disciples and eventually baptizing them. But surprisingly, Acts reports that when they baptized converts, they did so only in the name of Jesus. For example:

- And Peter said to them, "Repent, and be baptized every one of you in the name of Jesus Christ for the forgiveness of your sins; and you shall receive the gift of the Holy Spirit." (Acts 2:38, RSV)

---

34. Karl Rahner, "Trinity, Divine," *Sacramentum Mundi*, vol. 6 (Montreal: Palm Publishers, 1970), p. 295.
35. Adolph Harnack, *History of Dogma*, vol. I (Boston: Roberts Brothers, 1895), p. 79.
36. Charles Anderson Scott, "Baptism," *Dictionary of the Bible*, James Hastings, ed. (New York: Charles Scribner's Sons, 1909), p. 83.

• And he commanded them to be baptized in the name of Jesus Christ. Then they asked him to remain for some days. (Acts 10:48, RSV)

• On hearing this, they were baptized in the name of the Lord Jesus. (Acts 19:5, RSV)

The triadic formula is never once used at any baptismal event recorded in scripture.

Outside of the Bible, among the patristic works of the early Church, references to Jesus' "Great Commission" will sometimes lack the words "baptizing in the name of the Father, Son and Holy Spirit." For instance, Eusebius of Caesarea (265–339) was a bishop and a scholar of the biblical canon and is regarded as one of the most learned Christians of late antiquity. In his catalog of works, Eusebius frequently quoted from Matthew 28:19, yet twenty-one times he omits the triadic phraseology altogether, using instead either the form "Go, teach all nations in teaching them, etc." or "Go, teach all nations in my name, teaching, etc."[37] There is no mention of Father, Son, and Holy Spirit in the twenty-one occasions where Eusebius makes reference to the Great Commission. However, following the Council of Nicæa (325 A.D.), Eusebius uses the form of "Father, Son and Holy Spirit" on four occasions.[38] A possible explanation for why the triadic formula is missing from Eusebius' early works is

---

37. A second historical argument against the authenticity of Matthew 28:19 is summarized by church historians Jackson and Lake: "If Jesus' last words had been to order his followers to make disciples of all the Gentiles, would there conceivably have been so much trouble before the Apostles came to recognise the propriety of doing so? Would they have settled the point by an appeal to the story of Cornelius rather than to their experience on the mountain of Galilee? Would they have needed to hear the arguments of Paul and Barnabas before they paid attention to the commission of Jesus? Would the work of converting the Gentiles, which Jesus had given to Peter and the Twelve, have been entrusted to Paul, who had not been present on the Mountain, while Peter confined himself to preaching to the Jews, as Paul tells the Galatians? Would they have baptized, as Acts says that they did, and Paul seems to confirm the statement, in the name of the Lord Jesus—which is open to the gravest ecclesiastical suspicion, if not wholly invalid—if the Lord himself had commanded them to use the formula of the Church? On every point the evidence of Acts is convincing proof that the tradition embodied in Matthew xxvvviii.19 is late and unhistorical." (*The Beginnings of Christianity: Part 1, The Acts of the Apostles*, vol. 1, F. J. Foakes Jackson and Kirsopp Lake, eds. (London: Macmillan and Co., Ltd, 1920), pp. 336-7.

38. Kirsopp Lake, "Baptism (Early Christian)," *Encyclopædia of Religion and Ethics*, vol. II, James Hastings, ed. (New York: Charles Scribner's Sons, 1910), pp. 380-1.

that there existed manuscripts of Matthew's Gospel in the early part of the 4th century without the triadic formula. The theory is that Emperor Constantine's meddling in the Christological debate of 325 A.D. influenced how and what Eusebius wrote going forward. Unfortunately, we'll never know for certain the historicity of this verse, but clearly substantial evidence weighs against its authenticity.

For argument's sake, however, let us grant that Jesus actually gave the command to baptize disciples "in the name of the Father, Son and Holy Spirit." In doing this, must such words be understood as teaching the existence of three coequal "persons" within a single divine essence or being? According to the early Church, the answer is "no." Just as the book of Acts gives us a window into how the apostles understood the Great Commission, so too the early Church gives us a view into how Christians of the 2nd and 3rd centuries understood these words of Jesus.

I call as a witness a baptismal questionnaire (*interrogatio de fide*) preserved from the 3rd century, which reveals how references to the Father, Son and Holy Ghost were understood in a non-Trinitarian way:

> Dost thou believe with thy whole heart in God almighty, the Father, Creator of all things visible and invisible?—I believe.— And in Jesus Christ, His Son?—I believe.—Born of the Holy Ghost and the Virgin Mary?—I believe.—And in the Holy Ghost, one holy catholic (universal) Church, the forgiveness of sins, the resurrection of the body? And Palmatius (the candidate), moved to tears, cried: Lord, I believe.[39]

In this early baptismal creed, there is no detectable Trinitarian formula. It is not "the Father, Son and Holy Ghost in one essence" that the catechumen confesses as "God almighty." Rather, it is the Father *alone* who is confessed as "God almighty." It is the Father *alone* who is described as the "Creator of all things, visible and invisible." The Son is not only distinct from the Father, but the Son is distinct from "God almighty."

So even if we do accept the triadic formula in Matthew 28:19 as authentic, we do not find that the association of the terms Father, Son

---

39. Oscar Cullmann, *The Earliest Christian Confessions*, J. K. S. Reid, transl. (London: Lutterworth Press, 1949), p. 21.

and Holy Spirit requires an interpretation of three coequal, coeternal "persons" in one "being."

18: Pay Close Attention

1 John 5:7 and Matthew 28:19 have for centuries been considered the most important of the triadic passages for Trinitarians. This is because they are the only two passages in all of the Bible that feature the words Father, Son (or Word), and Spirit in close succession. Yet, there are other passages in the New Testament that contain what appear to be a divine triad. These passages, however, use a different set of words: *God, Christ* (or *Lord*), and *Spirit* (1 Corinthians 12:3-6, 2 Corinthians 13:14, Ephesians. 4:4-6, 2 Thessalonians 2:13-14, 1 Peter 1:2).[40] The most popular and succinct among these being 2 Corinthians 13:14:

> The grace of the Lord Jesus Christ and the love of God and the fellowship of the Holy Spirit be with you all. (RSV)

Easily overlooked—yet critical to recognize—is that with this triad variant we are no longer talking about the *Father, Son,* and *Holy Spirit.* Observe what the above verse *actually says* versus what it is *supposed to say* (according to the Trinitarian) but doesn't. I'll let Ware once more make the point:

> It is not here said that each is God, nor that all are equal, nor that all are to be worshipped, nor that all together constitute one. Therefore it does not teach the doctrine of the Trinity. Nay, it virtually denies it. For, as you observe, it does not speak of the Father, Son and Spirit, but of Jesus Christ and God and the Holy Spirit. Observe the difference, and consider what it implies. Would a Trinitarian express himself in these words and in this order, when intending to express his doctrine? If it were Father, Son and Spirit, we should of course regard them as three and not one, unless expressly instructed to the contrary; how much

---

40. One caveat is that sometimes these words are spread out over several verses.

more when the words run, Jesus Christ—and God—and the Holy Spirit.[41]

What is so easily overlooked by Trinitarians in their determination to find triads in the Bible is that these passages do not affirm a triad of *Father*, Son and Holy Spirit, but instead describe a triad consisting of *God*, the *Son of God*, and sometimes a Holy Spirit *of God*, (but at other times, just "spirit" with no definite article, e.g., 2 Thessalonians 2:13–14). Rather than describing a Trinity of three coequal "persons," these passages always reveal that the Son is distinct and set apart from *God*, and that it is the Father alone who is identified as God. Ephesians 4:4–6 is another such example:

> There is one body and one Spirit, just as you were called to the one hope that belongs to your call, one Lord, one faith, one baptism, **one God and Father** of us all, who is above all and through all and in all. (RSV)[42]

Though the words *Father*, *Son*, and *Spirit* are indeed found scattered within this collection of objects of faith, it is the Father alone who is identified as the "one God."

19: Paul

Despite Peter's remark in 2 Peter 3:16 that in all of Paul's epistles there were "some things hard to be understood," we find that when it came to the relationship between Jesus and God, Paul wrote very plainly and clearly. For example:

- "yet for us there is one God, the Father...." (1 Corinthians 8:6, RSV)

- "the head of Christ is God" (1 Corinthians 11:3, RSV)

---

41. Henry Ware, Jr., *Outline of the Testimony of Scripture Against the Trinity* (Boston: American Unitarian Assoc., 1832), p. 6.
42. Emphasis added.

- "And you are Christ's and Christ is God's" (1 Corinthians 3:23, RSV)

- "One God and Father of us all, who is above all...." (Ephesians 4:6, RSV)
- "there is one God, and there is one mediator between God and men, the man Christ Jesus." (1 Timothy 2:5, RSV).

20: Grace and Peace from God the Father, and...?

In each of his epistles, without an exception, Paul utilizes an opening salutation with his readers which appears in the form of "Grace and peace unto you from..." This salutation then always continues with terms unambiguous and unmistakable which distinguish between God, who Paul identifies always as "the Father," and Jesus, who is always identified as "Lord" (i.e., "the King/Master"). Moreover, in none of Paul's "Grace and peace from..." salutations will one ever find mentioned the spirit of God. Example, "Grace to you and peace from God our Father, and the Lord Jesus Christ" (Romans 1:7). This form of salutation, where God is unmistakably identified as "the Father," is repeated in 1 Corinthians 1:3, 2 Corinthians 1:2, Galatians 1:3, Ephesians 1:2–3, Philippians 1:2, Colossians 1:2, 1 Thessalonians 1:1, 2 Thessalonians 1:2, 1 Timothy 1:2, 2 Timothy 1:2, Titus 1:4.) Such consistent language makes it hard to argue that Paul was a Trinitarian, believing in three coequal persons in a single divine being.

21: God Subject to God?

Then comes the end, when he [Jesus] hands over the kingdom to his God and Father, when he has destroyed every sovereignty and every authority and power. For he must reign until he has put all his enemies under his feet. The last enemy to be destroyed is death, for "he subjected everything under his feet." But when it says that everything has been subjected, it is clear that it excludes the one who subjected everything to him. When everything is subjected to him, then the Son himself will (also) be subjected to the one who subjected everything to him, so that God may be all in all. (1 Corinthians 15:25–28, NAB)

At the end of the millennial Kingdom Age, even in his glorified state, when "Christ shall have put down all rule and all authority and power," Paul says that Jesus, the Son of God, will be made subject to not just the Father, but to *God* (v. 24). When all on earth has been reconciled, when the work of Jesus has been completed, Jesus is described as having a God over him, a God to whom he will be eternally subject to. This cannot be reconciled with the doctrine of the Trinity which posits that all three "persons" of the "Godhead" are coeternally coequal.

22: Around the Throne of God

In the book of Revelation, God is described in the context of seven "holy spirits" (Revelation 4:5), not one. In this same chapter, the glory of the Almighty God and Creator of all things is seen by John as sitting on a throne. In the very next chapter, a slain lamb, representing Jesus, stands before the One who sits on the throne. The lamb then takes "the [sealed] book out of the right hand of Him that sat upon the throne." A clear distinction is made here between the "Lord God Almighty" (the One on the throne), and the lamb who appears before the throne. All of this—the one Almighty on the throne, a lamb approaching the One on the throne, and seven spirits of God before the throne—is quite at odds with the mainstream doctrine of the Trinity where there are supposed to be "three coequal persons in one God." If we count and do the math here in an orthodox trinitarian fashion we do not find a trinity but rather an *ennead* or *noninity*.[43]

But irrespective of how one counts, the key point to recognize is that in chapters 4 and 5 of Revelation it is not the lamb but rather the One "who is seated on the throne" who is described as he "who lives for ever and ever" and before whom the twenty-four elders fall down and worship, casting "their crowns before the throne, singing, 'Worthy art thou, our Lord and God, to receive glory and honor and power, for thou

---

43. The Ennead or Great Ennead was a group of nine deities in Egyptian mythology.

didst create all things, and by thy will they existed and were created.'" It was only after it had been made perfectly clear to all that God was on the throne that the lamb then made his appearance, standing before the One who sat on the throne. The author's intention could not have been made more clear when it came to identifying and distinguishing between the lamb, here symbolizing Jesus, and God.

23: What's that Lack of Fuss All About?

There is something very odd *not* happening in the New Testament. There is no trace of any first century controversy about whether or not Jesus is God or that God is "tri-personal."

The conduct of the Jews toward the disciples after Jesus' death gives strong evidence that they knew nothing of any Trinitarian doctrine. The apostles were active in establishing a new dispensation of religion, and in the process brought on themselves the bad repute, abuse, and persecution of their countrymen. Wherever they went, they were assailed by the Jews with outrage and violence. They were accused of speaking blasphemous words against the holy place and the Law, of turning the world upside down, of designing to overthrow the religion of their fathers, and were scoffed at as followers of a messianic "king" who had died the ignominious death of a malefactor. But they were never accused of worshiping him or preaching him as God. Amidst all their enemies' accusations, they never brought forward charges that the apostles were preaching of more than one God, or of a tri-unity of "persons" within a "Godhead." And yet, in the eye of a Jew, such teachings would have been the most hateful things to their system. To teach that the deceiver from Nazareth, whom they had despised and slain, was the very God whom they had always honored and worshiped, the God of Abraham, Isaac, and Jacob!—nothing could have so excited them against the new religion and its active promoters. Yet it never formed the ground of their external opposition.

Internally, within the new community, the main New Testament-era controversies were about: 1) whether or not Jesus is God's Messiah (i.e., anointed king); 2) whether or not non-Jews could be fully acceptable to God without full Torah observance (e.g., circumcision, dietary regulations); 3) whether the dead in Christ will rise from the dead at

Jesus' appearing; 4) head coverings; 5) divisions within the churches on whether to follow Peter, or Paul, or Jesus; 6) speaking in tongues and spiritual gifts; and 7) what to do with sensual and sinning believers. But nowhere in the post-Gospel NT writings is there a whiff of any controversy about God being multi-personal or Jesus being God. One would think that something as controversial as the essence of God existing as three "persons," had it been a doctrine that was known to the first century Church, would have raised significant controversy, especially among Jewish believers. Ideas like the Trinity and God "becoming a man" are so foreign to Jewish thought and difficult to comprehend that one would expect a careful teacher like the Apostle Paul to address them constantly, yet nowhere in his epistles is there an example of him attempting to explain these inexplicable yet "essential mysteries" to his congregations. Nowhere does Paul discuss how the one God can be "three persons in one," or teach how in Christ Jesus "God became a man."

And would not such lessons have required constant repetition? Why then is there not even a single chapter dedicated to clarifying, let alone a single verse declaring the Trinity in all the New Testament? Could it be that the doctrine did not exist in the days of the apostles? And if it wasn't an essential doctrine and necessary for salvation in the days of the first century, then why does the mainstream insist that it is an essential and central doctrine of Christianity today?

24: A Trinity-free Pentecost

If the Trinity and deity of Christ are such core Christian doctrines, then how does one explain how three thousand devout Jews were converted by the preaching of Peter on the day of Pentecost and were "added to the church" and yet not one word about the Trinity or the "deity of Christ" or that "Jesus is God" was ever mentioned to them by Peter? Instead, Peter preached to them a Jesus who he described as "**a man approved** of God among you by miracles and wonders and signs, **which God did by him**" and that "**God hath made that same Jesus,** whom ye have crucified, both Lord and Christ" (Acts 2:22, 36, KJV).[44]

---

44. Emphasis added.

25: The Personification of the Spirit of God

When it comes to defending the Trinity, arguments related to the
Holy Spirit are inevitably left for last. The third person of the Holy Trinity, as the Holy Spirit is commonly referred to by Trinitarians, has always
been treated much like the ugly step-sister in the divine family of three,
for the Holy Spirit gets very little attention and when it does, it always
arrives as an afterthought and relatively little is said about it. Instead,
proof-texts pertaining to the "deity of Christ" make up the bulk of arguments when defenders of the Trinity do battle with non-Trinitarians. In
fact, debates about the Trinity almost inevitably turn into arguments
over "deity of Christ" proof-texts.

When attention is given to the Holy Spirit, it comes in the way of
two lines of argument. First, Trinitarians will argue that the Spirit is
called "God" in the Bible and therefore is God. For instance, John
Ankerberg and John Weldon, assert the following:

> The Holy Spirit is deity because He performs the functions of
> God, and because He is called God in Scripture.[45]

However, it does not follow that something must literally be God
simply because that thing is called "God" in the scriptures. Such an
inference requires the false premise that only God can truly be called
"God." Jesus made it clear that such logic is false when he responded to
the charge against him that he was making himself out to be God (which
Jesus flatly refuted), saying:

> Is it not written in your law, "I said, you are gods"? If he called
> them gods to whom the word of God came (and scripture can-
> not be broken), do you say of him whom the Father conse-
> crated and sent into the world, "You are blaspheming." because
> I said, "I am the Son of God"? (John 10:34–36, RSV).

In addition to men being called "God" in the OT when they serve
in the capacity of agents of God, such as Moses (Exodus 7:1), inanimate

---

45. John Ankerberg and Dr. John Weldon, *Knowing the Truth About the Trinity* (Eugene:
Harvest House Publishers, 1997).

things are called or referred to as "God" in the Scriptures. For instance, the city of Jerusalem is called "the LORD our righteousness" in Jeremiah 33:16. However, this doesn't make that city "God." Rather, it signifies that one day the presence and favor of God will be visible in Jerusalem. Angels of God are also repeatedly referred to as "God" or as "Yahweh/LORD" or speak as if they were God in the Scriptures, but that doesn't make them ontologically and literally "God" (cf. Genesis 16:9–10,13, 22:11–12, 31:11,13, 32:24,30, Exodus 3:2–6, Judges 2:1–4, 13:3,6,22).

Secondly, Trinitarians will argue that the Spirit is a "person" because personal actions and traits are sometimes applied to it in Scripture. For example:

> [...] the Holy Spirit is clearly not an impersonal force, as Jehovah's Witnesses claim, but a real person. He loves (Romans 15:30); convicts of sin (John 16:8); has a personal will (1 Corinthians 12:11); commands and forbids (Acts 8:29; 13:2; 16:6); speaks messages (1 Timothy 4:1; Revelation 2:7); intercedes (Romans 8:26); comforts, teaches, and guides into truth (John 14:26); and can be grieved, blasphemed, and insulted (Ephesians 4:30; Mark 3:29; Hebrews 10:29). Thus, once it is established that the Holy Spirit is a person, it is easy to see that the terminology in Scripture, such as His "filling us," or "being poured out," is not meant to imply the Holy Spirit is impersonal, but rather illustrates the intimacy of the believer's relationship to Him.[46]

The problem with this argument is that the Jews to this day apply the very same personal traits to the Spirit of God and yet they have never been confused to the point of believing that the Spirit is a "person":

> God's Spirit is always rather the extension of God's own personality, vitality and power, the very 'breath of his mouth' (Job 33:4; 34:14; Ps. 33:6; Wis. 11:20, etc.), not a second divine personal being. The 'Spirit of the LORD' is, in other words, a way of speaking of God himself, present and active: 'Spirit' is

---

46. Ankerberg and Weldon, ibid.

virtually synecdoche for 'God'. For this reason, the Spirit can readily be personified. Isaiah 63:10, for example, tells us that the wilderness generation 'rebelled, and grieved God's Holy Spirit'. But this (as the next line indicates) was simply a way of saying they grieved God himself, who was present in and through his Spirit. Indeed, this kind of personification of the Spirit in rabbinic Judaism occasionally goes even beyond that encountered anywhere in the New Testament, at least in the violence of the personal language used: as Abelson points out, the Spirit not only quotes Scripture, 'It also cries. It holds dialogue with God, or some person. It pleads. It laments and weeps; it rejoices and comforts.' But it would be entirely inappropriate to argue from this that rabbinic Judaism (or any other sector of Judaism for that matter) had come to think of the Spirit as an independent hypostasis distinct from Yahweh. Such language is simply figurative speech. [...] It is for this reason that it is quite inadequate, methodologically, to build a case for the divine personhood of the Spirit in the New Testament from those places where the Spirit is said 'to teach' (Lk. 12:12); 'to give utterance' (Acts 2:4); 'to say' (Acts 8:29; cf. 1:16; 10:19; 11:12; 13:2; 20:23; 21:4; 28:25); 'to send' (Acts 13:4); 'to forbid' (Acts 16:6); 'to appoint as overseer' (Acts 20:28), or whatever. All these could simply be shorthand for 'God, as Spirit (or 'by his Spirit'), said...', etc.[47]

26: The Lack of Evidence

Belief that "Jesus is God" has traditionally been the keystone of the doctrine of the Trinity, yet in the New Testament explicit references of Jesus being called "God" are very few, and even those few are generally plagued with uncertainties.

William Barclay, a Scottish author, radio and television presenter, Church of Scotland minister, and Professor of Divinity and Biblical

---

47. Max Turner, *The Holy Spirit and Spiritual Gifts* (Peabody: Hendrickson Publ., 2009), pp. 167–9. Turner is an evangelical and Baptist minister and was until his retirement in 2011, Professor of New Testament at the London School of Theology.

Criticism at the University of Glasgow, and who wrote a popular set of Bible commentaries on the New Testament that sold over 1.5 million copies, said this about the scripture evidence that Jesus is God:

> Here then is the sum total of the New Testament evidence for the application of the name God to Jesus Christ. In the first three Gospels Jesus is never called God. In the Fourth Gospel Jesus is unequivocally called God only in the cry of the adoring heart of Thomas (John 20.28).[48] There is no doubt that Paul thought of Jesus in terms of God, but there is no passage in his letters in which Jesus is called God beyond any doubt. In the General Epistles it is possible that Jesus is called God in I John 5.20, but by no means certain.[49]

John Behr, a British Eastern Orthodox priest and theologian who has served as the Regius Professor of Humanity at the University of Aberdeen and is the former Dean of St. Vladimir's Orthodox Theological Seminary acknowledges much the same:

> There are, however, several statements in Paul and the other letters, which might be read as describing Jesus as God (ὁ θεός), though in each case it is not a deliberate, unambiguous affirmation, but depends upon texts which are problematic in various ways, either in their grammar and translation or in establishing the correct text itself.[50]

Jesus never uses the term "God" for himself. No sermon in the book of Acts attributes the title "God" to Jesus. Over 170 times in the New Testament the Father is referred to as God. How many times is Jesus called "God"? Perhaps a handful of times, and in each case the text proposed has its difficulties. There is not in all the New Testament one passage which either asserts or implies that the disciples believed Jesus to have been God prior to his resurrection. Moreover, if the NT authors

---

48. See section "14: My Lord and My Elohim" on page 93.
49. William Barclay, *Jesus as They Saw Him* (Grand Rapids: Wm. B. Eerdmans Publishing, 1962), p. 32.
50. John Behr, *The Way to Nicaea Series: The Formation of Christian Theology*, vol. 1. (Crestwood: St. Vladimir's Seminary Press, 2001), p. 58.

believed it essential that Christians should confess and identify Jesus as "God" post-resurrection, how does one explain the nearly complete absence of this form of confession in the NT?

27: My Trinity Wasn't Their Trinity

The writings of the early church fathers of the second and third centuries left distinct proofs that they believed in something different than what is now taught as the doctrine of the Trinity. For them, the Son—regardless of however high a place of honor they thought was due to him—was still inferior to the one true God, who they identified as the Father alone. It is impossible to truthfully claim that these Christian writers embraced any scheme of the Divine Personality that is in harmony with any modern orthodox Trinitarian theory. Though many of the pre-Nicene fathers held to a theory concerning a triad of names (a collection of three things), their theological knowledge of what modern theologians describe as the Trinity was either absent or "imperfect."

For example, the first mention of the word *trias* (Greek for "three")[51] with reference to God is found in the writings of Theophilus of Antioch around 180 A.D. In narrating the Genesis creation, he refers to a group of three things: "God and his Word and his Wisdom"—a far cry from today's Trinity of Father, Son, and Holy Spirit.[52]

Others, such as Tertullian and Origen, later theorized about a different triad, one consisting of three divine beings, the founding "member" of which is God, who they identify as the Father. The other two "members" of their triad are less divine, one or both being derived from the first. Other early Christian writers confuse the two or blur them together into one:

> Consider the second-century writing 2 Clement, in which the proper distinction between Son and Spirit is confused in sayings such as the following: "Such a one then shall not partake of the

---

51. The Latin equivalent of *trias* is *trinitas* from which we get the English *trinity*.

52. Theophilus also wrote, "Therefore God, having his own logos innate [ἐνδιάθετον], that is in his own bowels, generated him, along with his own sophia [wisdom], vomiting him out before everything else." Jackson Lashier, *Irenaeus on the Trinity* (Leiden: Brill, 2014), p. 112.

spirit, which is Christ." Clearly, there is an equation here between the second and third persons of the Trinity. Other examples are not hard to find. Not surprisingly, the early documents mentioned above such as The Shepherd of Hermas are guilty of blurring the distinction between Son and Spirit; at times, it even conflates the two by stating that the "Spirit is the Son of God." Astonishingly, even the famous Apologist Justin Martyr opined that "[i]t is wrong, therefore, to understand the Spirit and the power of God as anything else than the Word, who is also the first-born of God."[53]

By the end of the fourth century, however, a triad of a different type supplanted the triads of Theophilus, Tertullian, Origen, etc. This new triad was something more akin to the concept of three "persons" in one divine essence, each one supposedly of the same substance with and coequal in glory to the other two. After much fierce debate in the latter half of the fourth century, this new doctrine was subsequently codified at the Council of Constantinople (381), a doctrine that its proponents now claim to be "the faith once delivered to the saints" (Jude 1:3), a doctrine commonly referred to as the doctrine of the Holy Trinity. Yet in the first 250 years of Christianity, it is clear that not one of the early Church fathers was acquainted with the orthodox Trinitarianism that has been handed down to us today.

The early nineteenth century German Protestant theologian, George Christian Knapp, confirms this assessment:

[W]e find, that Justin the Martyr, Clement of Alexandria, Origen, and other distinguished men of the Catholic party, made use of expressions and representations on this subject, which are both discordant with each other, and which differ totally from those which were afterwards established in the fourth century. [...] Athenagorus [,....] Novation [,....] Justin the Martyr [,....] Theophilus of Antioch, Clemens of Alexandria, and Origen [....] Tertullian [....] Thus it is obvious, that these philosophical fathers of the church, entertained far different

---

53. Veli-Matti Kärkkäinen, Christian Understandings of the Trinity (Minneapolis: Fortress Press, 2017), pp. 104-5. Kärkkäinen is a Finnish theologian, ordained Lutheran minister, and Professor of Systematic Theology at Fuller Theological Seminary.

views of the divinity of the Son and Spirit of which they often speak, than we do at the present time [....][54]

The words of the French Catholic bishop Pierre Huet are bit more critical, yet they still confirm the assessment that the early Church fathers were badly astray from what would later be viewed as "orthodox":

Many of the Christian doctors, who flourished before the Council of Nice, have spoken very incautiously concerning the mystery of the Trinity. The doctrine of Tatian, and of Justin, who was earlier than Tatian, as to the Trinity was not right. Pseudo-Clemens lies under the same accusation; as does also Theophilus of Antioch. Nay Tertullian and Lactantius, Clemens, Dionysius, and Pierius, all three of Alexandria, and many others have said unworthy and intolerable things upon this subject. Nor is it only in the doctrine of the Trinity, but in points also relating to the generation of Christ, and the procession of the Holy Ghost, wherein Tertullian and the greater part of the most ancient doctors preceding the Council of Nice, have equalled, if not exceeded Origen's, impiety shall I call it, or unskilfulness?[55]

Not only did these early Church fathers fail to develop a recognizably orthodox Trinitarian scheme, but only a few centuries later their writings on this subject would be considered heretical:

In the process of discovering the best way of stating the Christian doctrine of God, theologians like Justin Martyr, Irenaeus and Tertullian, who were in their day regarded as pillars of orthodoxy, held some doctrines which would have been regarded as rankly heretical two centuries later.[56]

---

54. George Christian Knapp, *Lectures on Christian Theology,* vol. 1, Art. IV, § 42, Leonard Woods, Jr., trans. (New York: G. & C. & H. Carvill, 1831), pp. 256, 298–300.

55. Pierre Daniel Huet, *Originis in Sacras Scriptvras Commentaria* (Rothom, 1668), Pref. p. 36, 45, apud James Yates, *A Vindication of Unitarianism* (London: Richard and John E. Taylor, 1850), pp. 259–60.

56. Anthony T. and Richard P. C. Hanson, *Reasonable Belief: A Survey of the Christian Faith* (Oxford: Oxford University Press, 1981), p. 172.

It is not an exaggeration to say that the Trinity, as defined in the systematic theology books of today, would have been something novel to the Church fathers of the second and third centuries.

28: Another Type of Shell Game: Whose Trinity Are We Now Talking About?

In the same line of thought as the previous point but moving away from the age of the Church fathers, it is today just assumed that when modern Trinitarians talk about the doctrine of the Trinity that there is a well-worded definition or theory that is universally understood and agreed upon, as if everyone is talking about the same thing. But this cannot be further from the truth.

In 2022, a discussion on this very point took place between Dr. Dale Tuggy and Dr. Steven Nemes,[57] two outspoken philosophers and theologians on the topic. Their conversation revealed one of the better kept secrets concerning the doctrine of the Trinity.

Nemes: Basically a Shibboleth is: you can tell a person is a member of a club if they talk in the right way. But if their accent is off, if their dialect is off, then you know they don't belong. That's what the Trinity is.

How can you have Jürgen Moltmann and Karl Barth both be Trinitarians when their pictures of God could not be more different than one another? And they don't agree on anything, and yet somehow they are both Trinitarians because they use the right words! That's all that it is. [...]

Tuggy: To me, [the Trinity] it's just been a massive fountain of confusion. It's widely avoided by laypeople and even by ministers. Like they don't want to touch it. It doesn't make sense to them. They feel stupid if they try to discuss it, even if they

---

57. From 2000–2018, Tuggy was Professor of Philosophy at State University of New York at Fredonia. Nemes is a Protestant theologian and phenomenologist who teaches Latin at North Phoenix Preparatory Academy.

have a seminary education. They still don't want to touch it, usually.

Nemes: And you would have to specify what Trinitarian theology, because like I was saying earlier, you've got Moltmann and Karl Barth are not the same, right? But they're both called Trinitarians, even though they could not differ more from each other and their doctrine of God. So even then you have to specify what Trinitarian theology [....]

Tuggy: Yeah. When they just say "the Trinity" or just "Trinitarian theology," I mean, I think that kind of presupposes that—that it's one view—but it really doesn't seem to be any.

Nemes: Exactly right. I think a lot of people, it's like, you know, one day you suddenly realize that even though you and your friends have been using the same words, you don't mean the same thing. But then, you know, you sort of wake up to the fact that you have these radical differences. People go through their lives—they hear about the Trinity their whole life—but when you sit down and [...] take a seminar on the Trinity in grad school, like I did [....] You read [William] Hasker—he doesn't say the same thing as [William Lane] Craig. Craig doesn't say the same thing as Moltmann. Moltmann doesn't say the same thing as [Karl] Rahner. Rahner doesn't say the same thing as Thomas [of Aquinas].

Tuggy: [Peter] van Inwagen... [and Michael] Rea.

Nemes: Yeah, exactly. Rea, for example. There are just so many differences among Trinitarian theologians, [...] they are not presenting one doctrine. What they are doing is they're taking a certain verbal formula from the Nicene-Constantinopolitan Creed and certain other stereotypical formulas, and they're trying to take that verbal formula and fit it within a greater system so that those words have a specifiable meaning. Basically, you take like a shell (which are the words), and fill the shell with something so that you have a Jello or a cake or whatever. They're trying to cook, basically with like a pan. They're trying to fill it with something, but they're not making the same product.

Like I was saying, you know, that there is no one doctrine of the Trinity. There are various verbal formulas that people take for granted as expressing the doctrine of Trinity. But those formulas are interpreted so differently among Trinitarian theologians that at the end of the day, like we were saying earlier, it's really just a Shibboleth. You prove yourself to be a member of the Trinitarian club because you try to make sense of these verbal formulas. But you don't have to have the same metaphysics at the end of the day as anybody else, which it seems to me is backwards.

Tuggy: Yeah. It seems weird in that it puts such an emphasis on verbal agreement and just parroting words that you don't understand. Whereas you would think that: no, it's the truth of the matter—that should be the main thing. But then there's not agreement.

Nemes: That's because this is a matter of authority at the end of the day. It's a matter of submitting and acquiescing to ecclesial authorities, which have decided that this is the way to go. [...] And it seems to me that fundamentally people who think that the Trinity is some non-negotiable for Christian faith, what they are doing is that they're taking the "appeal to the authority" as the fundamental mode of theological reasoning. And they think that being a Christian is fundamentally a matter of submitting to authorities. It's not about seeing that this stuff is true for yourself. It's not about being convinced in your own mind that these things are likely to be true. It's about submitting to authorities. And you let your submission guide your reasoning, and that's why people won't question these things or they'll insist on being a Trinitarian, even if you point to them the fact that there is no one doctrine of the Trinity. They'll say it doesn't matter. "This is what the Church teaches,

we have to believe it." That's religion as submission to authority.[58]

29: Can Someone Please Define a "Person"?

Trinitarians have been accustomed, for many centuries, to describe
the trinitarian "Godhead" with the use of the word *person*. For example,
theologian and Trinitarian apologist Roger E. Olson writes:

> First, what is the doctrine of the Trinity? Without getting into
> waters too deep, let's define it ecumenically and very generally.
> It is that God is one God eternally existing inseparably and
> equally as three "persons" (hypostases). But we must immedi-
> ately qualify that by saying that "person" here, in this doctrine,
> does not mean what "person" means in everyday American
> English. [...] We must explain that when we say three "per-
> sons" we do not mean "person" in the common, American
> cultural, individualistic sense. What we do mean is not clear.[59]

This lack of clarity is most evident when an inventory is taken of
the numerous ways in which Trinitarian theologians have tried to
explain what a *person* is in the traditional Trinitarian formulaic context.
"Just as there is nothing more humorous than philosophers trying to
define humor, so there is nothing more confusing than theologians trying to clear up the confusions of the Trinity."[60] And when it comes to the
meaning of the word "person," the endless babel of opinions would be
humorous if it were not so grievous.

For example, after a pastor initially explains to the unlearned man in
the pew that the Trinity is the union of three "persons" in a single Godhead, one who is more expert on the topic comes along and "clarifies"

---

58. Dale Tuggy and Steven Nemes, "Dr. Steven Nemes on Trinity Theories: Part 1," *Trin-
ities* podcast, episode 354 (September 19, 2022).

59. Roger E. Olson, "How Important Is the Doctrine of the Trinity?" *Patheos*, April 29,
2013, https://www.patheos.com/blogs/rogereolson/2013/04/1807/, accessed September 2, 2021.

60. Leonard I. Sweet, *New Life in the Spirit* (Philadelphia: Westminster Press, 1982), p.
33.

that the term "person" is misleading and that the Trinity should be understood as consisting of three *distinctions*, followed by another expert who proclaims it rather to be of three *diversities*, only to be interrupted by another teacher of mysteries explaining the Trinity to consist of three *subsistences* or *properties*, followed by a professor who sees here a single being of three *inseparable inter-personalities*, who is trailed by another who teaches that God consists of three *intelligent substances*, while another says: three *distinct cogitations*, three *distinct entities*, or three *distinct natures*. But others prefer the "persons" to be three *subsistent relations* (sometimes referred to as *external* relations or *internal* relations, take your pick), and yet others say: three *differences*, three *forms*, three *infinite minds*, three *hypostatic characters*, three *existences*, three *centers of consciousness*, three *active self-consciousnesses*, three *parts*, three *modes* or *aspects of being* or *existence*, three *functions*, three *special faces*, three *realities*, or three *"movements of life and love."* A few are bold enough to identify the "persons" as three *individuals*, or three *agents*, without realizing how close this is to tritheism. And finally, a few expositors with a straight face will step forward to clarify that the Trinity is actually a single being that consists of three "somewhats" or three "whos." But wait, there's more! The grandest of all explanations for how we should properly understand a "person" of the Trinity has been saved for last:

> A person is an impenetrable and divine mystery of a being, which is a substance possessing either aseity, or at least inseity, the essence of which is not only a supposit, but also a rational subsistence which makes it possible for it to lead a self-conscious and free existence as a self-standing, self-possessing and autonomous center of attribution; it is incommunicable, indestructible, and unique in its individuality, and in its positive transcendental relationship to being, to the ground of all being, to existence, and to becoming.[61]

I am not making this stuff up! This, sadly, is what these teachers call "explaining."

---

61. Petro Borys Tereshkowych Bilaniuk, *Theology and Economy of the Holy Spirit* (Rome: Centre for Indian and Inter-Religious Studies, 1980), p. 31.

Despite all of these varying opinions found buried within arcane books of systematic theology, never does the man in the pew come to learn from his instructors what I just shared: that according to the theologians and doctors of orthodoxy, the word *persons* in the definition of the "one God in three persons" doesn't actually mean *persons* as you and I commonly understand the word![62]

Adding to all the confusion is the fact that there are Trinitarian scholars who also refer to "God" (Yahweh) as a person,[63] which leaves us with a formula where God exists as "three persons (Father, Son, Holy Spirit) in one person (God)," instead of the typical text-book definition of the Trinity as "three persons in one essence" or "three persons in one being" as most orthodox theologians would put forward. At least one scholar recognized the conundrum and tried to solve it by "clarifying" that:

The word "person" does not have the same meaning in the two sentences which follow:

- God is three persons.
- God is a person.[64]

Such a solution, however, simply compounds the confusion, for the last thing the average Christian needs is an additional definition for the word *person* in this convoluted discussion about God.

When so many opinions are presented among Trinitarians themselves respecting their own doctrine, it only seems fair that the Christadelphians be permitted to entertain an opinion of their own, yet very different from all the rest, and that is, that the Trinity itself consists of error.

---

62. Wikipedia currently defines a *person* as "a being that has certain capacities or attributes such as reason, morality, consciousness or self-consciousness, and being a part of a culturally established form of social relations."

63. For example: "God is a person. [...] God, as a moral person, cannot be revealed by general laws [....] It is true, God as a moral person may be evidenced by [....]" (Truman M. Post, "The Incarnation," *Dickinson's Theological Quarterly*, vol. II, no. 1, James Kernahan, ed. (1876), p. 45). Post was a Congregational and Presbyterian minister, and was vice president of the Congregational Union. Post lectured on literary and historical topics, writing hundreds of book reviews for various publications and was awarded the degree of doctor of divinity by Middlebury College.

30: Unpersuasive and Untenable

Trinitarian theologian and author Dr. Fred Sanders, professor at Biola University, wrote a book in 2016 titled *The Triune God* which was addressed to his evangelical Trinitarian peers, and which was an attempt to "retrieve the riches of Christian doctrine for the sake of contemporary theological renewal." Despite his attempt to renew interest in embracing the historical understanding of the Trinity, he had to concede a few facts and face reality. He wrote:

> Indeed, the doctrine of the Trinity stands today at a point of crisis with regard to its ability to demonstrate its exegetical foundation. Theologians once approached this doctrine with a host of biblical proofs, but one by one, many of those venerable old arguments have been removed from the realm of plausibility. The steady march of grammatical-historical exegesis has tended in the direction of depleting Trinitarianism's access to its traditional equipment, until a prominent feature of the current era is the growing unpersuasiveness and untenability of the traditional proof texts that were used to establish and demonstrate the doctrine. 'Most theologians no longer expect to find in the New Testament a formal Trinitarianism, only an elemental Trinitarianism,' remarked conservative Jesuit theologian Edmund Fortman in 1972. The heightened historical consciousness of modern scholars has made the very idea that Trinitarian theology has a foothold in the documents of the

---

64. Alister E. McGrath, *Christian Theology: An Introduction* (Chichester: John Wiley & Sons Ltd., 2017), p. 178. Interestingly, on the very next page (p. 179), McGrath asks, "So what does it mean to be a 'person'? Our attention now turns to a modern philosophical analysis of the idea of a 'person' which is of considerable interest to Christian theology." Yet, through the remaining 300+ pages of his text, McGrath never provides a concise definition of the word "person," let alone two. Two definitions are required given that he acknowledged "person" is used in two different ways in his example above. McGrath *does* go on to discuss how the second century theologian Tertullian understood the word *persona*. This, however, doesn't help us today, for *person/a* as Tertullian understood the word no longer has the meaning it had in the second century. In the second century, *persona* was a "mask" used in theatre. Tertullian probably used the term with reference to these theatrical masks that were worn by Roman and Greek actors to indicate the various parts they were playing within a specific play.

New Testament seem laughable: 'Whatever Jesus did or said in his earthly ministry,' wrote R. P. C. Hanson in 1985, 'he did not walk the lanes of Galilee and the streets of Jerusalem laying down direct unmodified Trinitarian doctrine.' [...] A great deal of the assured results of modern scholarship in this area simply must be accepted, even when the result is the partial removal of the traditional way of demonstrating the exegetical foundation of Trinitarian theology. [...] The overall trend of sober historical-grammatical labors has been toward the gradual removal of the Trinitarian implications of passage after passage. Some of these proof texts evaporated because they were, in fact, never anything but Trinitarian mirages: 1 John 5:7's "three that bear witness in heaven," for example.[65]

31: The Christian Creed of a Sun-Worshiping Emperor

The convening of the Council of Nicæa (325 A.D.), where an agreement was reached upon what would become the orthodox definition concerning the nature of Jesus and God, was actually proposed (one might say "dictated") by the emperor Constantine the Great (who was unbaptized at the time). Constantine recognized that wrangling over religious matters (in this case, the identity of Jesus and God) was unhealthy for the state of his empire. In the 4th century, paganism was on the wane, and Christianity on the ascendancy. Historian Richard Rubenstein states that Constantine "agreed with Hosius [his chief advisor] that the dispute should be ended on terms favorable to Alexander and the anti-Arians." In other words, the outcome at Nicæa was predetermined by the emperor before the council was even convened; the only question: how to get there?

Rubenstein goes on to suggest why Constantine offered his personal hospitality to the bishops who he called to attend the meeting. Constantine had recently murdered his brother-in-law and nine-year-old nephew because they were a threat to his power. Hosting this conference could be seen as a positive distraction, shifting attention away from his recent misdeeds. So the bishops were invited to the emperor's home

---

65. Fred Sanders, *The Triune God* (Grand Rapids: Zondervan, 2016), p. 161.

at the emperor's expense, with their travel and living expenses for several months paid by Constantine.[66] Rubenstein also reveals that Constantine detested Judaism (as did many of the bishops), meaning that a Jewish understanding of God and of God's Messiah (the Son of God) were unlikely to have been part of the discussion at Nicæa.[67] Constantine's utmost desire was to establish a "New Rome," and he felt that Christianity could be used for uniting the divided empire. In other words, Christianity was being used as a tool of the State, and incredibly, the majority of the bishops permitted it!

The church historian Eusebius tells us that at Nicæa, it was the emperor Constantine who suggested that the creed incorporate the word *homoousios*, meaning "of the same essence," a word/concept not found in the New Testament and which had up to that point been used primarily by the Gnostics.[68] But it simply wasn't a term associated with Gnosticism, for it could also be found in the Hermetic tractate *Poimandres*—a pre-4th century syncretic writing in which Greek and Egyptian deities intermingled in world of Platonic thought.[69] If this wasn't bad enough, *homoousios* had been banned less than a century earlier at the Council of Antioch (268) due to its association with a Christological heresy. Considering all the baggage that accompanied this term, the fact that *homoousios* was suggested by Constantine, who himself at the time was a worshiper of the *Roman* sun god, Sol Invictus, tells us something about the influence that the emperor had over the hundreds of Church bishops who were present and how state politics had made inroads into ecclesiastical and doctrinal matters.[70]

Those bishops who believed that the Father and the Son shared the same "essence" embraced Constantine's new term, and those who did not were intimidated into going along with the suggestion. Only a

---

66. Richard J. Rubenstein, *When Jesus Became God* (New York: Harcourt Brace & Co., 1999), p. 71.

67. See earlier points 11 (Agency) and 12 (Jewish Preexistence), solutions which either were not known to the church fathers or else had been dismissed.

68. "The variety of its meanings and its previous association with Gnosticism—and, as Arius had pointed out, with Manicheism—made it suspect to the orthodox; [....]" Jaroslav Pelikan, *The Christian Tradition*, vol. 1 (Chicago: Univ. of Chicago Press, 1971), p. 202.

69. Kegan A. Chandler, *Constantine and the Divine Mind: The Imperial Quest for Primitive Monotheism* (Eugene: Wipf & Stock, 2019), pp. 107-8.

70. Ibid., pp. 78, 101-2.

handful of bishops protested the emperor's solution, and those few who disagreed with the term were quickly sent packing under threat of violence if they remained resistant to the Council's "consensus."

It is hard to imagine, but history shows that surrounding the Nicene council were crime, cover-up, dangerous ambition, and power-mongering, as well as fear, intimidation, intrigue, back stabbing, conniving, bludgeoning, and terrorizing.

The creed that emerged from Nicæa was a watershed for many other reasons as well. As Rubenstein observes, "While it looks forward to the ultimate resolution of the Arian controversy from the Catholic point of view [...] it also represents the last point at which Christians with strongly opposed theological views acted civilly towards each other."[71] When the controversy began, the bishops on whichever side of the controversy were inclined to treat each other as fellow Christians with mistaken ideas. But after Nicæa, Christianity changed. Rubenstein shares that:

> Constantine hoped that his Great and Holy Council would bring the opposing sides together on the basis of a mutual recognition and correction of erroneous ideas. When these hopes were shattered and the conflict continued to spread, the adversaries were drawn to attack each other not as colleagues in error but as unrepentant sinners and enemies of the empire: corrupt, malicious, even satanic individuals.[72]

As if this state of affairs were not bad enough, it gets even worse by the time we reach the year 381.

32: The Nicene "Spirit"

In the pivotal Nicene Creed (325 A.D.), all that was ever said about the Spirit of God (which would later be identified as the third "person" of the Trinity) was the following: "And I believe in the Holy Spirit." Period. End of sentence. End of Creed.[73] Never was the Spirit identified

---

71. Rubenstein, ibid., p. 87.
72. Ibid., p. 88.

as a "person," or called "God," or described as one-third of God's nature or His being, or recognized as coequal, coeternal, etc. Thus, the oldest creed that Trinitarians often claim as their own is actually not even Trinitarian, let alone binitarian. That creed is actually subordinationist unitarian in nature, with the Father alone being described as the "one God, the Father Almighty, Maker of all things visible and invisible," the Son as a derivative of that one God, and the Holy Spirit little more than a vague appendage and afterthought. Decades later, mainstream Christians still didn't know what to make of this Spirit. Even those who were considered orthodox on the divinity of the Son feared to call the Holy Spirit "God," partly because they doubted whether scripture justified such use of language, and partly because they feared appearing to confess a belief in three Gods. Gregory of Nazianzus, a prominent theologian of that day, openly admitted that mid-fourth-century theologians thought the Holy Spirit to be "a creature of God; others, God himself. Others say, they do not know themselves which of the two opinions they ought to adopt, out of reverence for the Holy Scriptures, which have not clearly explained this point."[74]

33: That Settled Nothing

Despite the Council of Nicæa's ruling, controversy over the nature of God and his Son continued for decades. The Roman Empire was in turmoil, and emperors and Augusti would come and go like the seasons. And with each new emperor, the Christological debate would change momentum. Before the 4th century was complete, successive emperors had taken alternating sides in the debate, each often banishing the key supporters of the opposing side and restoring back to favor those who had formerly been banished. Back and forth this game went. These political and military men used the Church to further their own ends, and constantly played one faction off against another. This tug of war, overseen by emperors, generals, and politicians, continued until the year 380.

---

73. With the exception of one anathema, which condemned all those who disagreed with the creed.
74. Gregory of Nazianzen, 380 AD, apud August Neander, *General History of the Christian Religion and Church*, vol. 2 (Boston: Houghton, Mifflin & Co., 1871), p. 467.

34: The General that "Settled" Everything

In January 379, a Spanish general by the name of Theodosius became co-Augustus of the eastern half of the Roman Empire. Out of political as well as religious motives, Theodosius energetically undertook to bring about unity of Christian faith within the empire.

At the time of his coronation, the followers of the Nicene Creed had regained the ascendancy, and a bishop who played a major role in Theodosius' faith, Ambrose of Milan, was a supporter of the creed. Then in the winter of 379, Theodosius fell gravely ill, so much so that in February 380 he sought baptism, hoping to have his sins forgiven before his death. That same month, without consulting the ecclesiastical authorities, Theodosius surprisingly issued a comprehensive edict defining and enforcing Nicene orthodoxy, one of the most significant documents in European history:

> It is Our will that all peoples ruled by the administration of Our Clemency shall practise that religion which the divine Peter the Apostle transmitted to the Romans [...] according to the apostolic discipline of the evangelical doctrine, we shall believe in the single Deity of the Father, the Son and the Holy Ghost under the concept of equal majesty, and of the Holy Trinity.
>
> We command the persons who follow this rule shall embrace the name of Catholic Christians. The rest, however, whom We judge demented and insane, shall carry the infamy of heretical dogmas. Their meeting places shall not receive the name of churches, and they shall be smitten first by Divine vengeance, and secondly by the retribution of Our hostility, which We shall assume in accordance with Divine judgement.[75]

The edict prescribing the Nicene Creed was to be binding on all subjects of the Roman Empire. Only persons who believed in the consubstantiality (same essence/*homoousios*) of the Father, Son, and Holy

---

75. Charles Freeman, *A. D. 381: Heretics, Pagans and the Dawn of the Monotheistic State* (Woodstock: The Overlook Press, 2009), p. 25. The original is found in the Theodosian Code, 16:I,2.

Spirit were henceforth to be considered true Christians by the State and the State's Church. Thus the "unity" among Christians, which emperor Constantine had vainly sought at Nicæa 55 years earlier, was ultimately imposed by fiat. The *Encyclopedia Britannica* notes concerning Theodosius' proclamation, that, "There is no doubt that the principle of religious intolerance was proclaimed in this edict." It is this spirit of intolerance that we still encounter within Christianity today.

Surprisingly, Theodosius recovered from his illness in the late spring of 380. It was natural for the emperor to attribute his recovery to God's favor on his edict, and as a zealous son of the Catholic church, he immediately began a purge of bishops who rejected the Nicene Creed. Theodosius went on to codify additional laws (enforced with severe penalties) which ensured that the Nicene Creed would suffer no rivals. Such laws included:

> In the name of our Lord Jesus Christ. [...] Since it has, moreover, come to our pious ears, that some persons have written and published ambiguous doctrines, which are not in absolute agreement with the orthodox faith laid down by the holy council of the holy fathers who assembled at Nicea and Ephesus, and by Cyrillus of blessed memory, once bishop of the great city of Alexandria, we order that such books whether written before or during this time, particularly those of Nestorius, shall be burned and delivered to complete destruction, so that they may not even come to the knowledge of any one. Persons who continue to have and read such writings or books shall be punished by death. Besides, no one shall be permitted as we have said, to acknowledge or teach any creed, except the one laid down at Nicea and Ephesus.[76]

---

76. *Corpus Juris Civilis* ("Body of Civil Law" from the Code of Justinian), Book I, Title I, "1.1.3. Emperors Theodosius and Valentinian to Hormisda, Praetorian Prefect." At Ephesus, in the year 431, a council of Christian bishops was convened by the Roman emperor. Known as the Third Ecumenical Council, the original creed of Nicæa (325) was reaffirmed along with an expansion of an article on the Holy Spirit (381)— describing the Spirit as "the Lord, the Giver of Life, Who proceeds from the Father, Who with the Father and the Son is worshiped and glorified, and Who spoke through the prophets."

In his book *A.D. 381*, Charles Freeman writes, "[...] it was the emperors who had actually defined Christian doctrine. This definition was then incorporated into the legal system so that orthodoxy was upheld by both secular and Church law, and heretics were condemned by the state. It is important to reiterate just how radical a development this was and the degree to which it diminished intellectual life. [...] The core of orthodoxy was, of course, the Nicene Trinity. Yet if the thesis of this book is right, this doctrine had only become orthodox because it had been enforced by the state."[77]

35: The Law: Dissenters Silenced

Theodosius' edict against non-Nicæans (non-Trinitarians), and the death penalty for non-conformists was incorporated into the Code of Justinian in the early in the 6th century. Penalties against non-conformists ("heretics") included:

> We purse them also by confiscation of their property [....] we leave to no one who is convicted (of such heresy) any power of giving, buying or selling anything or even of making contracts. The inquisition shall extend beyond death [....] Sons shall not become heirs, or enter upon an inheritance, unless they have abandoned the paternal depravity [....][78]

By the end of the century as the West slipped into the Dark Ages, the Code of Justinian was not in general use. But in the 11th century, the Code had a revival starting in Italy.

Despite the Code's temporary obscurity and modest revival, the prohibition against writing or speaking against the doctrine of the Trinity found its way across Catholic Europe, stretching even into England. An example can be found in The Blasphemy Act of 1697/98 (9 Will 3 c 35), an act of the English Parliament which made it an offence for any person, educated in or having made profession of the Christian religion,

---

77. Charles Freeman, *A.D. 381* (Woodstock: The Overlook Press, 2009), pp. 155, 164.
78. *Corpus Juris Civilis*, Book I. Title V. "Concerning Heretics and Manichaeans and Samaritans." Compare this sentiment and penalties with the worship of the "beast" in Revelation 13.

by writing, preaching, teaching or advised speaking, to deny the Holy Trinity. In England, one could not secure gainful employment if they were not a Trinitarian. Sir Isaac Newton kept his anti-Trinitarian views and writings private as a result of such laws. In Scotland, Thomas Aikenhead (1676–97) was tried under Scotland's Blasphemy Act and hanged on January 8, 1697, for allegedly denying the Trinity.

Such laws even found their way into the American colonies. In 1697, "An Act against Atheism and Blasphemy" was enacted in the Massachusetts Bay Colony prohibiting the denying of "the true God," which the article defined as "Father, Son or Holy Ghost." From 1819 to as late as 2003, a blasphemy law in the state of Maryland declared, "If any person, by writing or speaking, shall blaspheme or curse God, or shall write or utter any profane words of and concerning our Saviour, Jesus Christ, or of and concerning the Trinity, or any of the persons thereof, he shall, on conviction, be fined not more than one hundred dollars, or imprisoned not more than six months, or both fined and imprisoned as aforesaid, at the discretion of the court."[79] A similar Maryland law dates back to 1723. Delaware's constitution of 1776 required every public officer to take an oath professing faith in the Trinity. In Virginia in 1712, a public denial of the Trinity resulted in (for the first offense) "some severe punishment; for the second a 'bodkin should be thrust through the tongue'; if the culprit was incorrigible, he should suffer death." Even up to the Revolutionary War in 1776, denial of the Trinity in the Commonwealth could result in imprisonment and the loss of the custody of one's children.

It should go without saying that such laws have made it difficult for non-Trinitarian Christians to express their views without fear of punishment or death.

One of first Protestants who dared to publicly challenge the doctrine of the Trinity in writing was Michael Servetus. Despite the fact that the Protestant Reformation had condemned Catholicism, it failed to recognize that it had absorbed one of its core doctrines unchallenged: the Trinity. Orchestrating a sham trial, the reformer John Calvin had Servetus arrested in Geneva on account of this very theological issue.

---

79. "Article XXX: Crimes and Punishments," *The Maryland Code: Public General Laws,* Otho Scott and Hiram M'Cullough, compilers (Baltimore: John Murphy & Co., 1860), p. 208.

Before being burned at the stake at the direction of Calvin, Servetus held his ground in protesting against what he viewed as a corruption of the doctrine of God by Catholics and Protestant Reformers alike:

> To me [...] not only the syllables but all the letters and the mouths of babes and sucklings, even the very stones themselves, cry out there is one God the Father and [as a separate being] his Christ, the Lord Jesus. [...] Not one word [...] is found in the whole Bible about the Trinity nor about its persons, nor about the essence nor the unity of substance nor of the one nature of the several beings nor about any of the rest of their ravings and logic chopping.[80]

36: Who Needs Unitarian Apologists When We Already Have Trinitarians?

Seventeenth-century Enlightenment thinker, philosopher, and physician, John Locke, once noted:

> There is scarcely one text alleged by the Trinitarians which is not otherwise expounded by their own writers: [....][81]

What Locke was suggesting was that the doctrine of the Trinity could be disproved through a relatively simple exercise. Take each proof text used by Trinitarians to support the doctrine of the Trinity—be it John 1, Romans 9:5, Colossians 1:15–16, Titus 2:13, or any other passage—and broadly examine what Trinitarian commentators, expositors and scholars had already written concerning these verses over the centuries. Locke noted how in nearly each case, for each proof text put forward, one would find a respectful number of dissenters within the

---

80. Roland Bainton, *Hunted Heretic, The Life and Death of Michael Servetus, 1511–1553* (Boston: Beacon Press, 1960), p. 24.
81. From note in a commonplace book of John Locke entitled "Lemmata ethica, argumenta et authores 1659" in Bodleian Library, MS. Locke d. 10, p. 177, with the heading "Unitarian." Also found in *The Life of John Locke: With Extracts from His Correspondence, Journals, and Common-Place Books*, vol. 2, Lord King, ed. (London: Henry Colburn and Richard Bentley, 1830), p. 103.

Trinitarian camp who would argue *against* the orthodox interpretation, and do so for solid reasons—be they exegetical, grammatical, lexico-graphical, contextual and/or logical.[82] These dissenters would not be of Socinian, Arian, or Unitarian persuasion, or liberal humanists, but rather they would be mainstream Protestant and Catholic clerics and theologians who have found serious fault with the traditional, orthodox interpretation. If Locke's observation is correct—that each of the passages used by Trinitarians to argue for the existence of a Triune god, or for the deity of Jesus, can be disarmed and reasonably dismissed by Trinitarians themselves—then what actually is holding up the trinitarian edifice? It would appear, little more than tradition and intimidation.

37: Essentially Unessential

According to the standard bearers of orthodoxy, the doctrine of the tri-unity of God is an essential component of the Christian faith. In order to be a Christian, nay, in order to be saved, defenders of Trinity teach us that one must embrace a belief in one God existing in three "persons," or to be more precise, three distinctions subsisting in one essence. For example, a contemporary Evangelical pastor is emphatic as to the essentiality of believing in the Trinity:

> Question: Can you become a Christian if you deny the Trinity?

> Answer: I would answer, "No." If you don't believe in the Trinity, then you don't understand who God is. You may say the word "God" but you don't understand His nature. Second, you couldn't possibly understand who Christ is—that He is God in human flesh. The Incarnation of Christ is an essential component of the biblical gospel, as John 1:1–14 and many other biblical passages make clear. To deny the Trinity is to

---

82. Attempts to prove the accurateness of Locke's observation can be found in the works of a few authors. See e.g., John Wilson's *The Concessions of Trinitarians* (Boston: James Monroe & Co., 1845) and most recently, *Commentaria Contra Trinitatem: The Epistle to the Hebrews* (Poole: New Covenant Press, 2023).

deny the Incarnation. And to deny the Incarnation is to
wrongly understand the true gospel.[83]

According to this belief, the doctrine of the Trinity is so essential
that rejecting it affects your salvation, as another contemporary Trinitarian scholar explains:

> The Trinity is the very object of our saving faith. Therefore,
> the church fathers and apologists thought that belief in the
> Trinity is essential to our salvation.[84]

Another contemporary voice endorses this opinion, although he
curiously contradicts his predecessor when it comes to the early church.
For one says that the essentiality of the Trinity was known to the "church
fathers and apologists," yet our next voice says that the early church
didn't know what to make of the doctrine of the Trinity (despite the
necessity of embracing its formula):

> So if you're denying the doctrine of the Trinity, you, you're in
> deep water. I don't even think you're saved. Okay? However,
> there's a lot of people who misunderstand the doctrine of the
> Trinity, you know, they just believe that Jesus is their God and
> Savior and they're trusting him for their salvation and they've
> really never given it much thought. Well, you need to do your
> homework. But I'm sure there's gonna be quite a few people
> kind of confused about the Trinity, because even the early
> church wasn't quite sure what to make out of it.[85]

This same expert also says:

> Let me say this. The doctrine of the Trinity is clearly taught in
> the New Testament. Okay? To deny the doctrine of the Trinity

---

83. John MacArthur, "Can You Be a Christian and Deny the Trinity?," *Grace to You*,
    https://www.gty.org/library/questions/QA519/can-you-be-a-christian-and-deny-
    the-trinity (accessed May 8, 2022).

84. Jay Rogers, *Why Creeds and Confessions?* (Clermont: Media House International,
    2016), p. 92.

85. Phil Fernandes, "Christian Beliefs 1–Trinity," lecture given at Institute of Biblical
    Defense, Bremerton, Washington on January 23, 2012.

is to deny what the Bible clearly teaches about the nature of God. Okay?[86]

However, a 19th century Episcopalian takes exception regarding the doctrine's "clarity":

> The doctrine of the Trinity, a doctrine the knowledge of which is certainly necessary to salvation, is not explicitly and evidently laid down in Scripture, in the Protestant sense of private interpretation.[87]

But at least they all agree on the "essentiality" of the doctrine to one's salvation. And yet despite the emphasis these men place on the doctrine and the position to which it is elevated, an encounter with the real world exposes a concerning and embarrassing truth:

> I have said for decades now that I would be fearful to give a quiz, a test, at the vast majority of Evangelical churches this coming Lord's day, on the doctrine of the Trinity, for fear that probably 70 to 90% of the people who've actually made the effort to go to church would fail that quiz—they would fail that test—and would test positive for some kind of heresy.[88]

This state of affairs is easily confirmed by other Trinitarian ministers, who confess:

> The problem is, of course, that many, perhaps most, Christians have little or no understanding of the doctrine of the Trinity. And they couldn't care less. I once was a member of a church with the word "Trinity" in its name. During the eight years I attended there faithfully I don't think I heard a single sermon on the Trinity. And I am almost sure that had I polled

---

86. Ibid.
87. Archbishop John Hughes (Q.) and Thomas S. Bacon (A.), *Both Sides of the Controversy Between Roman and Reformed Churches* (New York: Delisser & Procter, 1859), p. 469.
88. James R. White, "Is the Trinity Essential? And Much More," *YouTube*, February 11, 2020, https://youtube.com/watch?v=qtYnEr_EJOw, accessed October 10, 2022.

the congregation few would have been able to express, let alone explain, the doctrine of the Trinity.[89]

It doesn't take years or decades for an Evangelical Christian to come to the same conclusion, for anyone who has witnessed a "crusade" or "revival" knows that "getting saved" never involves any mention of the Trinity, despite its supposed essentialness for salvation. Just call as a witness the "sinner's prayer," which is taught as a confession that brings lost people into the family of God. Examine this prayer that penitents are urged to repeat and you will find absent the doctrine of the Trinity:

> Dear Lord Jesus, I know that I am a sinner, and I ask for Your forgiveness. I believe You died for my sins and rose from the dead. I turn from my sins and invite You to come into my heart and life. I want to trust and follow You as my Lord and Savior. In Your Name. Amen.[90]

Though it is claimed to be an essential element to being a Christian, the Trinity is rarely mentioned to new converts to Christianity. Within Protestant churches, knowledge of this doctrine is typically "learned" by osmosis, often through Bible footnotes or through hymns, rather than through intentional instruction.

> And it's so interesting, because, even though you know, I was raised in the church, and I raised my family in the church, and we were very, very involved in, you know, ministry and Bible studies and Sunday school, I cannot remember a time when there was a lesson or—you know, perhaps there was and I just

---

89. Roger E. Olson, "How Important Is the Doctrine of the Trinity?," *Patheos*, April 29, 2013, https://www.patheos.com/blogs/rogereolson/2013/04/1807/, accessed September 2, 2021.

90. https://en.wikipedia.org/wiki/Sinner's_prayer As an aside, none of the commonly used sinner's prayers make any reference to the word *Christ*. Christadelphians would point to this apparently minor detail as another example of the departure of mainstream Christianity—or at least the Protestant varieties—from the New Testament Gospel message. The apostle John noted in John 20:31 that everything he wrote was so that the reader would recognize and confess Jesus as the *Messiah* (*Christ*). Not only is the word *Christ* missing from these prayers, but the meaning and significance of the word is almost always missing from the message that precedes these prayers.

don't have perfect recall—but I don't recall a time when from the pulpit or from a Sunday School lectern that I was ever taught about the doctrine of the Trinity. It's just things that you absorb, through comments or things that are said from the pulpit. But no one ever, I don't recall ever a sermon saying, let's sit down and find the scriptural basis for this doctrine that we base our faith on. I can't ever remember that happening.[91]

Those who are of Roman Catholic tradition fare better, for the doctrine of the Trinity is presented to catechumens, albeit briefly, and in what could be described as little more than a shell or formula. For example, in the *Baltimore Catechism*, volume 1, there are less than ten short sentences in the entire book which introduce the doctrine of the Trinity, several of which simply admit that the Trinity is a mystery and cannot be understood by mortals. The one attempt that the *Catechism* makes at making sense of the Trinity results in this analogy:

We may compare the three Persons in one God to three persons in a human family: father, mother and child.[92]

This analogy, unfortunately, yields tritheism—a belief in three gods.

So when we step back and compare the words with the practice, what we have, at least within the Protestant world, less so in the Roman Catholic tradition, is a doctrine that is declared to be essential in theory, but in practice, is treated as a non-essential.

38: Finally, No Verses

We would know very little about God without the Bible, for the Bible is God's revelation of Himself to humankind. It is through the Bible that we learn who God is, what God is like, and what God does. It is important to our salvation to learn what God reveals about himself in

91. Hildy Chandler, "Mother Disrupted—Hildy Chandler (Part 1)," *Unitarian Christian Alliance* podcast, episode 2, November 23, 2020.
92. Bennet Kelley, *The New Saint Joseph Baltimore Catechism*, no. 1 (New York: Catholic Book Publishing, 1964), pp. 19–20.

the Bible. It is also important to note what the Bible does *not* say about God. In light of the topic of this chapter, let us note what the Bible does not say about the Father, the Son, and the Holy Spirit. For instance,

- There are no verses in the Bible that define God as being Father, Son, and Holy Spirit.

- There are no verses in the Bible that reveal God as three, three in one, or as a grouping of "persons," "distinctions," "properties," "substances," "relations," "forms," "modes," etc.[93]

- There are no verses in the Bible that say that the Father, Son, and Holy Spirit are coequal.

- There are no verses in the Bible that say that the Father, Son, and Holy Spirit are coeternal.

- There are no verses in the Bible that say that Jesus has or had two natures, two minds, or two wills.

- There are no verses in the Bible describing Jesus as a God-man, as fully God and fully man, or as half God and half man.

- There are no verses in the Bible where Jesus declares that he is God.

- There are no verses in the Bible that describe Jesus as "God the Son."

- There are no verses in the Bible that call Jesus "eternally begotten."

- There are no verses in the Bible describing Jesus as being uncreated, unlimited, infinite, almighty, omniscient, or as existing from eternity.

- There are no verses in the Bible that instruct us to pray to Jesus.

- There are no verses in the Bible that identify Jesus as an Old Testament angel, or which associate Jesus with an Old Testament theophany, or which assert that any "God" or "Lord" perceived in Old

---

93. See p. 96.

Testament times was in fact a literally pre-existent, pre-human Jesus.

- There are no verses in the Bible where the Holy Spirit is worshiped or which say that the Holy Spirit is to be worshiped.

- There are no verses in the Bible where the Holy Spirit is an object of prayer or which say that the Holy Spirit is to be prayed to.

- There are no verses in the Bible where the Holy Spirit is identified as having a personal name.

- There are no verses in the Bible where the Holy Spirit engages in a back-and-forth conversation with anyone.

- There are no verses in the Bible where someone gives thanks to the Holy Spirit.

- There are no verses in the Bible that include the Holy Spirit in a greeting or salutation (see p. 104).

- There are no verses in the Bible that say that it was necessary for God to die in order for us to receive forgiveness of sins.

- There are no verses in the Bible that say God died or that God can die.

- There are no verses in the Bible that say that God can be tempted to sin.[94]

- There are no verses in the Bible that say that we must believe that Jesus is God in order to obtain eternal life.

- There are no verses in the Bible that say that we must believe that God consists of three "persons" in order to obtain eternal life.

---

94. Refer to Jesus' forty-day temptation in the wilderness (Matthew 4:1–11, Mark 1:12–13, Luke 4:1–13).

Closing Thoughts

Though in no way exhaustive, these are just some of the types of arguments that Christadelphians might put forward to justify their rejection of the mainstream doctrine of the Trinity.[95] Many more could be enumerated, but this book is not intended to be a dissertation on Biblical Unitarianism, a history of the doctrine of the Trinity, or a critical commentary covering all of the proof-texts used to defend this doctrine. One may not agree with their dismissal of what is commonly viewed by the mainstream as a central doctrine of Christianity, but the reader can at least better understand why Christadelphians, as sola scriptura biblicists and Restorationists, have chosen to reject the orthodox doctrine of the Trinity in favor of what can be described as an early, first century, low Christology. They believe that their position is more consistent with Peter's original confession of faith, the confession upon which Jesus' church was to be built. They have therefore chosen to avoid Christological dogma tainted, as they believe, by state interference, Catholic (and Protestant) tradition, human philosophy, metaphysical speculation, and unintelligible mysteries. With respect to the identity of Jesus, Christadelphians believe that there is an alternative answer that doesn't resort to tritheism, modalism, Arianism or Unitarian Universalism,[96] and (which most importantly to them) can be supported by Scripture.

---

95. The bulk of this chapter (i.e., the numbered sections) exists as a standalone volume, written by the same author but under a different pen name. See *Little Known Facts About the Trinity* (Poole: New Covenant Press, 2022).

96. Biblical Unitarianism is not the same thing as Unitarian Universalism. The latter is the result of the former's near century-long slide into extreme liberalism, transcendentalism, social humanism, religious inclusivism, and a fear of formal creeds, at the beginning of the 20th century. There still remain groups of *biblical* Unitarians throughout the world who uphold the primacy of scripture and who reject these characteristics of modern Unitarian Universalism while at the same time rejecting Arianism, modalism, tritheism, universalism, and Oneness Pentecostalism.

CHAPTER 7

Intolerance

Tolerance is the positive and cordial effort to understand another's beliefs, practices and habits without necessarily sharing or accepting them.[1]

—Joshua L. Leibman

If your opponent defeats you in an argument, all is not lost; you can still call him names.[2]

—Elbert G. Hubbard

"ANTI-CHRIST," "DECEIVERS," "DOGS," "false prophets," "false believers," "false Christians," "falsifiers of the Gospel," "cursed," "damned," "condemned," "monsters," "slippery snakes," "babblers," "rascals," "heretics," "idolaters," "infidels," "traffickers of chicaneries and vile absurdities," "frenzied persons," "maniacs," "enemies of Christianity," "worshiping Satan," "worshiping demons," "their destiny is eternity in hell with Satan and his demons," and "it's better that they be thrown into a pool with something tied around their neck." These are not my words. This litany of epithets come directly from the mouths and writings of Trinitarians describing individuals or groups who deny and reject the doctrine of the Trinity.[3] And, of course, the epithet "cult" is also a part of this collection.

It is remarkable how much the 4th century spirit of intolerance permeates these epithets. Yet this is what one often encounters when today's mainstream Christians come into contact with those who disagree with the doctrine of the Trinity. At its heart, the controversy is over the answer to a single, straightforward question that Jesus presented to the disciple Peter some 2000 years ago: "But who do you say that I am?"

---

1. Joshua L. Leibman, *The New York Times*, February 17, 1952.
2. *The Communist*, vol. 1, no. 3 (August 2, 1919), (Chicago: Federation-Michigan Alliance), p. 3.
3. *The Encyclopedia of Trinitarian Quotes* (New Covenant Press), forthcoming.

(Matthew 16:15). Peter's response: "You are the Christ, the Son of the living God."[4] It is the same response that Christadelphians today would give if presented with the same question. Strangely, Peter's response to Jesus no longer finds the same approval that it once did.[5] Instead, something more sophisticated is needed, more in line with the 4th century Nicene Creed which professes that Jesus is "very God of very God ... begotten of the Father before all worlds ... begotten, not made, ... being of one substance with the Father."[6]

Rejection of this newer and "improved" formula is sufficient cause to call down imprecatory curses and fire upon the head of the hapless "heretic." We can thank 4th century bishops and Roman emperors for much of this mess, along with an endless line of Christians who have perpetuated these attitudes for more than seventeen centuries.

One of the first examples of this type of intolerance against "incorrect dogma" is found in the closing anathema of the Nicene Creed of 325 A.D.,[7] which found its full expression in imperial laws enacted in 381 by Emperor Theodosius who used them to enforce uniformity of belief among all Christians.[8]

---

4. The bishop of Durham reminds us, "So, when Peter says to Jesus 'You are the Messiah', and when Caiaphas says the same words but as an ironic question, neither of them should be understood as either stating or asking whether Jesus thinks he is the incarnate second person of the Trinity. Subsequent Christian use of the word 'Christ' (the Greek translation of 'Messiah'), and indeed of the phrase 'son of god', as though they were 'divine' titles has, to say the least, not helped people to grasp this point; but grasped it must be if we are to understand Jesus in his historical context." (N. T. Wright, *Jesus and the Victory of God*, vol. 2 (Minneapolis: Fortress Press, 1996), pp. 485-6.) See p. 78.

5. "And Jesus answered him, 'Blessed are you, Simon Barjona! For flesh and blood has not revealed this to you, but my Father who is in heaven.'" (Matthew 16:17)

6. Philip Schaff, *The Creeds of Christendom*, vol. 1 (New York: Harper & Bros., Publishers, 1877), pp. 27-8.

7. Which reads: "But those who say: 'There was a time when he was not;' and 'He was not before he was made;' and 'He was made out of nothing,' or 'He is of another substance' or 'essence,' or 'The Son of God is created,' or 'changeable,' or 'alterable'— they are condemned by the holy catholic and apostolic Church."

8. See page 128. The power of the emperor was such, and the crises that faced his empire so immense, that he chose to endorse one faction of Christians, the supporters of the Nicene Creed, over its rivals. Through edicts he then isolated a class who thenceforth were to be described as "heretics," resulting in the suppression of freedom in religious thought and dissent that has lasted for more than a millennium.

It is not surprising why Theodosius supported the Nicene party over rival views. The Nicene formula of Father, Son, and the Holy Spirit being of co-equal majesty represented the majority belief in his home-land of Spain. But there are other reasons why he may have been drawn to favor the Nicene cause. As historian Charles Freeman enumerates:

> The first is that the elevation of Jesus into full divinity fitted better with the current authoritarian zeitgeist. There were immense difficulties in finding a place within the ideology of the empire for a Jesus who was executed as a rebel against Rome. Second, the Goths and other tribes that Theodosius was fighting had been converted to Christianity at a time when the Homoian faith[9] of Constantius had been in the ascendant, and they were to cling to this faith for decades to come. By creating a religious barrier between Homoian Goth and Nicene Roman, Theodosius could define a fault line along which he could rally his own troops against 'the barbarians'. In the west, in these same years, Ambrose of Milan was stressing the relationship between support for the Nicene faith and the success of the empire in war.[10]

As Freeman goes on to explain, Theodosius had no theological background of his own and he was unaware of the intractable problems that were bound to occur when he incorporated Nicene dogma into imperial law. Specifically, the emperor's laws would silence the Christo-logical debate on the identity of Jesus and his relationship to God when these matters were still unresolved within the Church. If discussion had been allowed to continue among Christians, a broader consensus might have been established over time, one that could have preserved freedom of debate as well as a reasoned basis for any agreed formula.

Unfortunately, Theodosius chose to suppress all alternative beliefs on the Christological question, making an abrupt break with the policy of toleration upheld as recently as the 370s by his co-ruler in the west, Valentinian II. Freeman believes that it was likely that Theodosius was frustrated by the pressures he found himself under and genuinely believed that an authoritarian solution would bring unity to the

---

9. The rival Christological view of the Trinitarian Nicenes which held the views of Arius.

10. Charles Freeman, *A.D. 381* (Woodstock: The Overlook Press, 2009), p. 103.

embattled empire. However, by deciding the "correct" view himself and outlawing alternative Christian opinions, the emperor crossed a watershed. The result made it acceptable—and legal—for Christians to persecute other Christians. The opportunity for debate which once existed among the various factions of Christians was totally squelched and in its place dropped the hammer of intolerance and terror, and physical persecution at the hand of the State against "heterodox" opinions.

Today, Christians no longer burn heretics at the stake along with their writings, or confiscate their property on account of incorrect dogma. Nonetheless, the spirit of intolerance often surfaces and burns within the hearts of the defenders of orthodoxy when this "core teaching" of Christianity—the Trinity—is challenged or rejected. This brings us full circle back to the word *cult* and how it is misused by mainstream Christians today.

Christian aggression in the form of physical violence against heretics may be a thing of the past, but verbal aggression on account of the heterodoxy of a person's doctrinal beliefs is still commonplace. And when it comes to triggering the aggression of mainstream clerics and laity alike, there's nothing comparable to a person rejecting the doctrine of the Trinity. Whether encountering non-Trinitarians in person, or more commonly in passing, the result is often the application of anathemas, name-calling, slander, fearmongering, excommunication, and use of the "c" word against the non-Trinitarian.

As many Christadelphians and Biblical Unitarians can attest, it's as if you are assaulting Jesus and blaspheming God when it is discovered that you do not believe that Jesus is ontologically or literally God in the flesh, or that you reject the formula of "three co-equal, co-eternal persons in one God." A common line of argument goes, "Who do you think you are, and how dare you question these things? The Nicene and Athanasian Creeds have been around for centuries! Why are you questioning the first article of our church's statement of faith? You must be a really prideful person!" Truth be told, an atheist—someone who rejects God— would receive a warmer welcome within most mainstream churches than someone who rejects the Trinity. Christadelphians are only trying their best to make sense of the Bible and find it unnecessary to resort to Greek philosophy and metaphysics to correctly answer Jesus' question to Peter.

Don't Touch the Stuff!

Within "orthodoxy," when a person rejects the Trinity, it is often the case that the individual will be accused of having been brainwashed by a cult. Likewise, any group that rejects the Trinity will be marked as a cult, and called out as threat to the eternal salvation of others. This is how I reacted when I first encountered the Christadelphians nearly 40 years ago. Looking back, I have wondered what it was that taught me to respond in such a way. The short answer: other Christians of my own tribe taught me to think that way. For certain it wasn't the Bible. It was the pastors and authors who warned me not to trust those who denied the doctrine of the Trinity. No, you shouldn't even wish them "God-speed" (2 John 1:10). Or as one Baptist pastor recently put it: "Burn the books! . . . I'm telling you, burn the stuff! Get it out of your house, get rid of it!"[11] This was the type of message that was conveyed to me back then. This was how I learned to distrust any point of view that did not conform to the orthodox theology that I had been taught.

I had been conditioned by my pastors, the radio preachers who I regularly listened to, as well as the evangelical authors and commentaries that I read, to think this way of others who didn't share our understanding of Jesus and the Trinity. Trinity-deniers were evil, not to be trusted. The unspoken message was that you shouldn't spend time listening to what they had to say for fear of succumbing to their lies and their twisting of Scripture. You risked losing your salvation if you got too close to them. "You're going to go to hell if you don't believe that Jesus is God," was the worry. I was being conditioned how to think and how to respond to a Trinity-denier as a result of peer pressure, loss of independent thinking, tradition, distancing myself from outsiders, blind acceptance of mysterious revelations, and an endorsement of contradictory ideas (doublethink).

In retrospect, this is quite ironic. If you refer back to Chapter 2, you will see that these are some of the characteristics of a cult! The fearful attitude that says, "Hey, you can't talk to anybody about this doctrine or question it," "Don't talk about it in public," "Don't think about it," "Don't question what we teach you," "We are the experts," "We know best, even

---

11. Brian Wilson, "Guarding the Faith," sermon delivered at Victory Baptist Temple, Piedmont, Missouri, on June 27, 2021.

if this doesn't make sense..."—such thinking and attitudes are what cults push on their members to keep them tightly within their control. In several ways, I had fallen into a cultish mindset.

Part of the problem is that many people within mainstream churches treat the words and teachings that come from the pulpit as words and teachings coming more or less directly from the mouth of God. When we believe that our pastors and leaders are "filling in for God," we automatically believe and accept the messages and so called "truths" that descend from the pulpit. This conceptual framework produces staunch followers who have an uncompromising, unwavering devotion to their particular denomination, their particular church, and their particular leaders and their teachings. All too commonly attached to this framework is a rigid dogmatism that displays itself in an unwillingness to honestly listen and genuinely consider another person's point of view. And when it comes to the matter of the Trinity, it goes beyond just a matter of refusing to listen. Rigid dogmatism can turn to a visceral fear or hatred of the other party. Five hundred years ago, espousing non-Trinitarian views would have resulted in persecution and death of the offender.[12]

Today, it is rare to find a Biblical Unitarian or Christadelphian using any of the litany of epithets that opened this chapter against their Trinitarian opponents. Historically, there is no question that Trinitarians have been more aggressive and hostile when compared with non-Trinitarians Christians. This may be because Trinitarians have much more to lose. Imagine the great embarrassment if Trinitarians, like the king in the folktale, were to realize they have been parading around in the buff for more than a millennium! Trinitarian intolerance may therefore be an aggression born of insecurity. Perhaps it is also due to arrogance derived from the position of power which this party has held for seventeen centuries.

These facts should be of great concern to every zealous defender of the Trinity since Jesus warned his followers that they would be the ones who would be persecuted, not the ones doing the persecuting, (see

---

12. It is worth noting that you will not find a single historical instance of an anti-Trinitarian Christian sentencing or putting a Trinitarian to death on account of their religious beliefs.

Matthew 5:10-12; 24:9; Luke 6:22-23; John 15:20; 1 Thessalonians 3:4; 2 Timothy 3:12).

Confessing Jesus as the Christ

There is a lot of disparaging labeling going on out there by Trinitarian Christians against non-Trinitarian Christians. My hope is that as a result of reading this book we will all be more cautious when we are tempted to apply the label of "cult" to individuals and the groups they belong to. Especially when we pause to consider such verses such as:

Who is the liar but the one who denies that Jesus is the Christ? ... No one who denies the Son has the Father; everyone who confesses the Son has the Father also. (1 John 2:22–23, NRSV)

God abides in those who confess that Jesus is the Son of God, and they abide in God. (1 John 4:15)

Who is it that conquers the world but the one who believes that Jesus is the Son of God? (1 John 5:5)

Whoever has the Son has life; whoever does not have the Son of God does not have life. I write these things to you who believe in the name of the Son of God, so that you may know that you have eternal life. (1 John 5:12–13)[13]

Do these verses sound like they condemn non-Trinitarian Christians? Every Christadelphian unhesitatingly confesses, as Peter did, that Jesus is the Christ, the Messiah, the Anointed of God, the Son of God— in other words, the future king of Israel and eventually king of the whole world. For this is, after all, what these titles signify (see Psalms 2, Mark 15:32, John 1:49). How certain can we be, therefore, that Christadelphians and other non-Trinitarians who identify themselves as Christians do not possess the "eternal life" that John here speaks of? Perhaps Trinitarians should reconsider and think more soberly before hurling epithets at others who profess Jesus as the Christ.

---

13. Where is the third person of the Trinity in these verses?

Conclusion

As we have seen, using the word *cult* is an easy way to criticize a group, but often a poor way to describe one. The problem is that when people hear the word *cult*, discussions end before any study has even begun. Why is this? Is it possible that we use this label to condemn others in order to keep things simple, clean, easy, and plain for ourselves?

I strongly believe that we need more discussions with others who think differently from ourselves, for how else will we ever learn whether our current positions are correct or the best ones to hold? If you never take the time to listen to a different point of view, how can you be sure that your beliefs are indeed true?

This problem reminds me of what is written in the book of Proverbs:

> The first to present his case seems right, till another comes forward and questions him.[14]

You will always, *always* seem to be in the right if you never allow another person an opportunity to question your position, or if you take the attitude that your theological beliefs are right simply because you were "lucky" enough to be born into the "right" Christian denomination. Sadly, it is easier to suspect non-Trinitarians of sinister motives and dismiss them as "anti-christs" than it is to talk to them and actually listen to a different point of view. And by *listening*, I don't mean *debating*. It is hard to actually hear what your opponent is saying if you are instead thinking up responses to what they are saying while they are still speaking.

Based upon my own experience, I believe that many who dismiss the teachings of others, do so not so much because the teachings are self-evidently false, but because the teachings are simply unfamiliar and that they have been fearmongered into believing that this "new" teaching (at least new to them) will jeopardize their salvation, or perhaps cost them their job or status. Rather than allowing themselves to be challenged by the thoughts and ideas of others and of other Christian

---

14. Proverbs 18:17, NIV.

traditions, they often dismiss other viewpoints because they are too lethargic or fearful, or even too prideful, to be challenged intellectually.

Yes, there are dangerous teachings out there. Yes, there are ravening wolves seeking sheep. I am not advocating that you be gullible and believe everything you read and hear. Don't forget to refer back to the 23 characteristics of a cult as described in Chapter 2 to help keep you away from danger on your journey.

What I am advocating here is not to blindly accept everything that you come across, but rather to take the time to actually examine and "try the spirits" and as Paul put it, to "test and prove all things [until you can recognize] what is good; [to that] hold fast." (1 Thessalonians 5:21, Amplified).

Apathy is found among those who do not care to stretch their intellectual muscles and are content to leave honest reflection and the challenging of one's own perspectives to the "experts." Indifferent persons are susceptible to inadvertently believing whatever world-view and ideology their upbringing granted them, whether these beliefs are based on reality or not. Since such individuals do not care one way or the other, they will always remain the same, be that for better or worse.

But as a reader of this book you have taken a bold step in another direction. Unless you happen to be a Christadelphian who picked up this book out of curiosity, just to see what someone is saying about your denomination, the fact that you've made it this far into this book says a lot about your willingness to listen and learn about others. I tip my hat to your tolerant and inquiring spirit.

The purpose of this book is not to convince you to join a Christadelphian fellowship or suggest that you leave your current faith community. Rather, I hope to encourage you to go further, to open your mind, turn off the TV, put down the phone, read broadly, investigate deeply, think critically, compare multiple points of view, ask questions, show some skepticism, don't be afraid to challenge traditions, listen attentively, and be willing to learn from others. If you wish to keep arms length from Christadelphians and their ilk, that's fine. It's your choice. But what isn't fine is remaining ignorant to a different point of view, especially when you haven't even investigated fully what you yourself believe on some of the topics raised in this book. Ignorance may be bliss, but it certainly isn't a virtue.

Beginnings

He that would make a real progress in knowledge, must
dedicate his age as well as youth, the latter growth as well as
the first fruits, on the altar of truth.[1]

—GEORGE BERKELEY

L ITERALLY MEANING "island of sand," Sable Island is little
more than a sliver of dunes covered with marram grass poking
out of the Atlantic Ocean. Situated 190 miles (300 km) off the
coast of Nova Scotia, it sits astride the great circle route from North
America's east coast to Europe. No more than a mile across at its widest
point, the crescent-shaped island has the somber moniker of "Graveyard
of the Atlantic," with more than 350 recorded shipwrecks occurring
along its shores, at the cost of over 5000 lives. It was here that a pivotal
event took place in the spring of 1832.

Departing from London on the 18th of May, the good ship *Marquis
of Wellesley* was a teak and copper-bottomed vessel with three mainsails.
Her destination was New York City. On board was a young man named
John Thomas (b. 1805) who was emigrating to America ahead of his
father. Serving as the medical attendant for the 89 passengers aboard,
the voyage was an important link in the chain of events that determined
his career along with the emergence of the Christadelphians.

No sooner had the ship set sail and reached the open sea than bad
weather set in which lasted throughout the long and tedious journey.
For two weeks the ship was driven by unfavorable winds and rough seas
before the main-mast snapped, and along with its spurs, was carried off
by the waves. The ship was now at the mercy of the boiling sea and the
passengers were badly frightened by their plight. Many turned religious
and pressed the captain to organize a service by which they might
implore the mercy of God and his assistance. The captain consented. To

---

1. "Essay on Tar-Water," *Siris* (1744).

the Doctor fell the task of reading a chapter from the Bible, followed by a public reading of a published sermon. The people were temporarily calmed, though the ocean's fury was not.

Due to the cloudy conditions, nautical observations could not be taken, consequently the location of the ship remained uncertain. The ship's captain felt confident that he knew where he was, but Dr. Thomas expressed his doubt. One Sunday, the doctor looked out his cabin window and was struck by the appearance of the water. He left his room to remark to a crewman that given her present course, the ship would run aground. He was mocked and informed that a medical doctor could know nothing about the matter, being a landsman. Upon this rebuke, the doctor returned to his room. It wasn't long afterward, however, that the ship scraped the bottom and then struck heavily several times, forced down each time by the waves. The cry went out, "Breakers ahead!" The ship crashed against the bottom twelve times while passengers screamed and crewmen went about excitedly following the captain's orders, laboring to get the ship turned about and back out to sea.

In the midst of the bedlam, the doctor had to deal with a male passenger who he found sprawled out on the deck, and who was shouting out in terror, "We shall go to the bottom! We shall go to the bottom!" Thomas calmly pointed out that they were already at the bottom and couldn't get any lower than at the present. Not wanting to alarm others, he kept it to himself that he feared the prospects were high that the ship would soon break up.

Though he was far from being irreverent or irreligious, Dr. Thomas had up to this point in his life never made religion a matter of practical interest. Uncertain as to his fate at that moment, not to mention the question of any afterlife should he die at sea, he concluded that if he ever got to shore again he would make it a priority to seek God with his whole heart and be led by the truths as taught in the Bible.

Eventually the captain's efforts succeeded in getting the ship turned around, but almost as soon as he had, the vessel struck bottom again. Water was rushing in at various places and repairs were hurriedly performed. These efforts succeeded in keeping the ship afloat, but pumps had to be employed throughout the remainder of the journey. It was a harrowing eight weeks after departing from London that the *Marquis of Wellesley* finally arrived at its destination.

Making Good on a Promise

Upon disembarking, Dr. Thomas did not forget the resolution he had made to seek God with earnest. He made use of letters of introduction provided by the president of the Baptist Bible Society of New York and another Baptist preacher, both of whom he had met upon docking, the former asking where he planned to settle. Dr. Thomas replied that he was going to Cincinnati, to which he was told that the people of that region were very hospitable but sadly were "very much infected with Reformation"—a reference to the teachings and religious movement then led by Barton Stone and Alexander Campbell, both Presbyterian ministers.

Upon arriving in Cincinnati, he met Major Daniel Gano, who was a clerk of the Supreme Court of the United States and part of the religious reformation that was taking place at that time. Gano took a kind and sincere interest in the Doctor, and when the Major learned of the events that he encountered at sea, and that he was looking to find the truth about God and the Bible, he introduced Dr. Thomas to Walter Scott who was one of the religious leaders of the area. Walter Scott made a sudden and significant impact upon Dr. Thomas' life, giving direction to his thinking and further reason to pursue his spiritual goals. Gano, discovering that Dr. Thomas identified as Christian but that he had never been baptized (outside of infant baptism), rushed him into making a decision to be immersed. This event, however right it seemed to Dr. Thomas at the time, was later regretted on account of its hastiness.

Alexander Campbell

Shortly after this baptism, Dr. Thomas was introduced to Alexander Campbell, the leading preacher of the Restoration Movement. Campbell, who often liked to test a man's mettle, could see potential in the young man and subsequently urged him to give public addresses to a number of his churches. Though the Doctor was initially irritated over this imposition, feeling himself inadequately prepared for the task, Campbell refused to back down, and so the Doctor relented. Despite his initial lack of enthusiasm to preach, Dr. Thomas was surprised to find that the audiences responded favorably to what he had to say. Even in light of this success, Dr. Thomas felt he was being pressed into a work for which he was utterly unqualified, and quickly decided to head east, accompanied by additional letters of recommendation from Campbell.

His circuitous journey eastward included stops at Baltimore and Philadelphia before turning southward to Richmond. To his chagrin, at each location, he found himself being wheedled into public speaking on religious matters, his reputation preceding him. It was his original intent to devote himself to medicine, but these events forced Dr. Thomas to dedicate an increasing amount of his time and energies into scriptural study at the expense of his professional occupation.

The Doctor as an Author

As these events show, Dr. John Thomas' entrance upon a new theological career path was "accidental." Another unexpected event—this one encouraged by a Campbellite pastor at Philadelphia—led Dr. Thomas to embark on a writing career. The suggested enterprise was the publishing of a new monthly religious periodical, *The Apostolic Advocate*. In its prospectus, he explained that he had "neither sympathies nor antipathies to gratify—having no gift, or 'sacred office' of pecuniary emoluments to blind the eyes, to pervert his judgment, or to distort his mental vision—being interested in upholding no religious dogmas, in sustaining no sect, in pleading for no sectarian creed [....]"[2] After receiving the endorsements of a sufficient number of subscribers and the support of Alexander Campbell himself, the periodical was begun, first appearing in May of 1834.

Dr. Thomas' writing around this time was described by a Philadelphia journal in the following manner: "style chaste, reasoning close; takes high ground; treats all human authority very unceremoniously; appeals directly to the Scriptures." That he was a well-read man was evident from his familiarity not only with Milton, Newton, Gibbon, Mosheim, and the English poets, but also with the early Christian fathers.

Before the publication of the second edition, Dr. Thomas left Philadelphia and carried out his intention of settling in Richmond, Virginia.

---

2. John Thomas, "Proposals...," *Apostolic Advocate*, vol. 1, no. 1 (1835 reprint), p. 2.

When he arrived, a meeting-house there which had no pastor called upon him to occupy its pulpit, offering in exchange a salary. He remarked on the matter in the *Advocate*:

> [...]the securing of our services as an Evangelist was agitated among the brethren. But concerning this, our mind was and is made up. If any community of brethren "desire to be at charges *with us*" we should not so much object to receive the donation; but to become a hireling, and to have our pay, and so forth, discussed at co-operation meetings at the bar of the church and the world, being unscriptural and degrading, we cannot, away with it.[3]

The Doctor told the Richmond brethren that he would rather live on bread and cheese and maintain his independence of thought and action, than submit himself to the power of committees and trustees. This stance led him to return to the practice of medicine for his own support, while at the same time carrying on the publication of the *Advocate*.

Unwelcome Questions

His independent spirit soon led him into trouble, for only two years after their introduction, the friendship between Dr. Thomas and the periodical's chief supporter, Alexander Campbell, began to cool. Dr. Thomas objected to how many of the Baptists who were being allowed to join the Movement were doing so without being re-baptized. The debate had scarcely begun to die down when a new controversy was ignited between the two. The cause was a collection of 34 questions that were published in the *Advocate* in December 1835, under the heading "Information Wanted," of which the general tenor was mostly to question the doctrine of the immortality of the soul, a doctrine taken for granted by the Campbellites in common with most of their

---

3. John Thomas, "Alleged Cause of the Troubles in Canada," *Apostolic Advocate*, vol. v, no. 3 (July 1838), pp. 92–3.

contemporaries. Also questioned was the meaning and significance of the kingdom of God and its place in the gospel message.

Not having arrived at conclusions himself concerning these questions, Dr. Thomas had hoped that by publishing them he might receive the aid of others. He was wrong. The reception accorded to these questions was very unfriendly and even hostile. Readers began canceling their subscriptions, and he was beset on every side by those who vented their ill humor by calling him an "infidel." "Our mind was not made up on any of the questions," he later wrote, "we wanted light; we asked for bread, but our contemporaries gave us a stone."[4] Elsewhere he reflected:

> No one that we are aware of ventured to touch fairly and candidly on a single point or suggestion contained in them. [...] And why have they done so? Is it because it is a criminal thing [...] to ask for information?[5]

The cry raised against Dr. Thomas and his questions was beneficial in that, as he later shared,

> Had no notice been taken of these questions, it is exceedingly probable we should have thought no more about them. [...] Instead of intimidating or putting us to silence, it only roused our determination to comprehend the subject; if wrong to get right, and, when righted, to defend the right, maintain the right and overthrow the wrong, or perish in the attempt.[6]

An Attempt to Disfellowship

Alexander Campbell's response was of bitter chagrin, leading to a rebuttal in his own periodical, the *Millennial Harbinger*, in which he tried to refute Dr. Thomas' questions and paint him as a sectarian speculator. Additional articles on the controversy followed from the *Harbinger*, to which Thomas made exhaustive replies. The result was that the

---

4. John Thomas, "Transition from Error to the Truth," *Herald of the Future Age*, vol. 3, no. 6, p. 125.
5. John Thomas, *The Advocate*, vol. 5, no. 11 (May 1838), p. 4.
6. *Herald of the Future Age*, ibid.

feelings of antagonism between the two men which had for some time been growing reached a full-scale rupture.

More moderate members within the Movement were greatly disturbed by the conflict and a mutual friend proposed a truce between the parties. Both agreed. But the agreement was short-lived when Campbell resumed his public criticisms of Thomas' views. Then in 1837, Campbell went so far as to publicly advise Dr. Thomas' church to disfellowship him and to urge the sister churches within Campbell's sphere of influence to do likewise, declaring:

> [...] it therefore belongs to the church of which he is a member to consider whether his (Dr. Thomas') case is not of the same genus with that of Hymeneus and Philetus (2 Tim. ii. 16,17) and then for sister churches to set upon their approbation or disapprobation of her decision upon this question.[7]

The church to which Dr. Thomas belonged found Campbell's demand distasteful and felt that the latter was holding "a rod of terror" over their heads and tying their hands, for they feared that if they were to acquit the Doctor of the charges they would be judged harshly and publicly denigrated in Campbell's *Harbinger.*

They nonetheless examined the matter and found nothing worthy of disfellowship concerning the conduct or beliefs of Dr. Thomas. They admonished him to tone down the rhetoric and the degree of sharpness expressed in his public responses to Campbell, hoping that this would help all parties involved. They also expressed in writing that they felt Campbell was using his prominence and influence within the Restoration Movement to punish someone who openly disagreed with him over matters of doctrine and practice. Though they feared their response would result in their own disfellowship within the Movement, Thomas' church held its ground.

Not far from Dr. Thomas' home church, another church decided to wade into the controversy. They likewise found Campbell's demand for disfellowship distasteful and uncalled for. In a long letter they responded

---

7. John Thomas, "The Church at Paineville and the Harbinger", *The Advocate*, vol. 4, no. 9 (January 1838), p. 209.

to Campbell's challenge, hoping to identify the specific point of conten-
tion between the parties.

> A short review of his (Thomas') alleged "abominable"
> doctrines, we ask first to be allowed to take. To our minds, the
> grand foundation question promulgating the negative of
> which, brother T. has been reprobated as a materialist,
> branded as an infidel, and denounced as unworthy of the
> name of Christ; we say, to our minds, the main fundamental
> question is this: was there at the beginning, when the "Lord
> God formed man of the dust of the earth, and breathed into
> his nostrils the breath of life, and man became a living soul," a
> substance created, which was not matter, annexed to an
> organized body composed of dust of the ground, and which
> was from the moment of its creation to be necessarily,
> essentially, absolutely, and unconditionally, immortal and
> indestructible, and which should subsist for a time,
> independent of the organized matter to which it had been
> annexed, in a disembodied conscious state? [...]

> We have been taught by some of the prominent actors in this
> reformation [movement] to call "Bible things by Bible names,"
> and that as words represent ideas, if the words are not in the
> book, neither are the ideas. The inspired Moses records the
> simple account above of man's beginning, the sentence
> pronounced upon him for his transgression—"dust thou art
> and unto dust shalt thou return"—and its execution, 930 years
> from his creation: "he died." Nowhere in Moses' history of
> Adam's creation and death can we find a "Thus saith the Lord,"
> which taught him that he had an immortal spirit within him,
> that would, when his body should return to the dust, exist for
> ages in a disembodied, conscious state [....]

> In the absence of such authority, brother T. feels himself
> bound to hold the position he does, which is the negative, and
> from which it follows, as an inseparable consequence, that
> man, without Jesus Christ, the resurrection, and the life,
> perishes as the brute.[8]

For many today, looking back a century and a half later, this dispute may seem blown out of proportion. But to Dr. Thomas, the dispute went to the heart of one of the essential doctrines of Christianity: the resurrection and the reward of the dead. For if mankind has within itself an immortal element that continues in conscious existence after death, flitting off to celestial bliss to join the company of angels, then what is the purpose of the resurrection of the dead that Jesus repeatedly spoke of and promised to the faithful? It would be unnecessary.

William Tyndale (1484–1536), martyr, and translator of the first printed edition of the English Bible, highlighted what was at stake in his words to the pope's champion in England at that time, Thomas More. Tyndale pointed out to More:

> And ye [Catholics], in putting them [the departed immortal souls] in heaven, hell, and purgatory, [ye] destroy the arguments wherewith Christ and Paul prove the resurrection [of the righteous] [....] And again, if the souls be in heaven, tell me why they be not in as good case as the angels be? And then what cause [purpose] is there of the resurrection?[9]

The question is a valid and important one. Likewise Dr. Thomas felt that the issue merited discussion. The problem was that he and Campbell could not agree on an answer, and moreover, Campbell feared that further discussions on the question would threaten and undermine his reformation and unification efforts, causing schisms throughout the body.

Unsurprisingly, the controversy grew even greater, with individuals and churches taking positions on the doctrines in question, as well as with Campbell's "bull of excommunication" against Dr. Thomas. Campbell boasted in print that Thomas' "followers" could surely be no more than a dozen in number throughout the entire middle-eastern section of the United States, and that perhaps only one out of one thousand readers of the New Testament could even follow the Doctor's position.

---

8. Robert Roberts, *Dr. Thomas: His Life and Work* (Birmingham: C. C. Walker, 1911), pp. 131–2.
9. William Tyndale, *An Answer to Sir Thomas More's Dialogue*, Parker's 1850 reprint, Bk. 4, ch. 4, pp. 180–1.

Campbell, however, was overstating the facts. In a reply to Campbell, Dr. Thomas clarified the matter:

> My "partizans," [sic] as you term some of the brethren whom you fellowship, are not only "very, very few," but as far as I know, absolutely *not-existing*. There is not a single brother within the range of my personal acquaintance, that I could *venture* to call my "partizan." The brethren know, and can testify, that I have never made a single effort, or manifested the least disposition to make a partizan. [...] No, no; to head a party has no charms for me. I know too well the inconstancy of men's allegiance to their leaders; I am too well acquainted with the fickleness of humanity, to propose to myself any such bauble as an object of ambition.[10]

John Thomas had not wanted to preach or teach the Bible, or to be the editor of a religious periodical, let alone solicit followers, form partisans to his name, or break off into yet another denomination or Christian movement.

Later that year, Dr. Thomas was cordially invited to visit some of the sister churches in central Virginia, which he gladly was willing to do. At each stop, any prejudices against him were quickly removed from the minds of many when they had an opportunity to hear his side of the controversy. Several encouraged him to take advantage of a planned visit to the area by Campbell later that year to renew a friendly cooperation between the two. Dr. Thomas expressed his willingness.

When Campbell arrived in Richmond in October of that year, Dr. Thomas went to hear him preach. Unfortunately, Mr. Campbell spent two hours preaching and railing against him and his "speculations and untaught questions" and lumped Thomas into the same league with infidels. The Doctor calmly held his peace while listening to this attack and even stepped forward after the lecture to respectfully greet his attacker. It was agreed upon by both that it might prove beneficial to spend a few hours in private discussing the matters between them. After three hours of discussion between the two, the question was asked of the Doctor what he proposed as a solution to their difficulties. Dr. Thomas

---

10. Thomas, "Letter Third," *The Advocate*, vol. 4, no. 9 (January 1838), p. 315.

responded, "I propose that you write upon whatever you please, and advocate whatever you please, I will do the same, and leave the public to judge: without you attacking me or me attacking you." This reasonable suggestion, however, was not to Campbell's liking. "Oh, but that won't do; you cease to write upon these things altogether," was Campbell's response.

Campbell's unyielding stance towards the Doctor may have been the result of the former's inflated estimation of himself. Campbell had expressed to others that he felt that God had called him, not by an audible voice, but by divine providence—just as he believed God had called Martin Luther, John Calvin, and John Wesley—to become the supervisor of the reformation then taking place in the central and western states of America, and that he, therefore, had a right to say who should be his co-laborers.[11] Acting on this right, he rejected Dr. Thomas for his failure to align himself with this calling, and for threatening with schism the new popular ecclesiastical system that Campbell was "supervising." The age difference between the two did not help matters either, with the former being twenty years younger, and from a theological perspective, a novice in the eyes of Campbell.

Moving West

Several months after this discussion, Dr. Thomas decided to leave Richmond, recognizing the backward state of affairs that existed in Virginia. A relative in Illinois had encouraged him to relocate, stressing to him the advantages that could be derived by moving west. After first spying out the land, he decided to move his family to Illinois, arriving there in 1840. The distribution of the *Advocate* had to be suspended in the process, and no other publication took its place. Although the printing press was brought along, no immediate use could be found for it.

Thomas purchased 288 acres of land 33 miles (53 km) northwest of Chicago and farming became his new livelihood. Things did not go as smoothly as he had hoped, however. After the price of wheat plummeted and difficulties arose in securing dependable labor, the "medical doctor turned farmer" quickly changed his opinion of agricultural life.

---

11. Roberts, ibid., pp. 148–9.

Within less than two years, he decided to return to civilization, and in St. Charles, Illinois, made preparations to begin a local newspaper. Within a year of its start, the newspaper was sold and the Doctor embarked on a new writing venture, this time editing a religious monthly which was to replace the suspended *Advocate*.

Concurrently with the publication of his new periodical, titled the *Investigator*, Dr. Thomas gave himself to the public teaching of the Bible whenever opportunities presented themselves. At St. Charles he would often be invited to speak publicly by a group of Universalists whose meeting place was just across the street from his lodging. They frequently needed someone to fill in for their traveling preacher and thought to inquire of his willingness to speak. He agreed, but only on the condition that he would be exempt from their preliminary worship service, for he did not recognize them as Christians but thought no harm could come from simply expounding the Bible to them, which included challenging their belief that all men will eventually be saved. The Universalists never directly attacked the Doctor's views, though they would do so indirectly by inviting others to come debate him on occasion.

In 1843, he needed to return to Virgina to collect a debt owed to him for a farm that he had left behind. Upon arrival, he visited a Campbellite meeting house in Fredericksburg and was recognized there and asked if he would be willing to speak that Sunday. Similar invitations to give Bible lectures were received from other parts of Eastern Virginia once it was learned that Thomas had returned to the region. Unfortunately the debt owed to him for the farm could not be collected, and he decided to leave for home, stopping first at Louisville, Kentucky, where there too, he was asked several times to speak and debate.

Returning to Trouble

Dr. Thomas' stay in Kentucky lasted longer than expected, and for a period of a year, he was given frequent opportunity to speak at a Campbellite meeting-house, much to the chagrin of some of its members. In 1844 his plans changed again, and he returned to Richmond where he began a new religious periodical, *Herald of the Future Age*, the title reflecting Thomas' increasing recognition that the event of Jesus' future reign on earth was a key part of the truth of the Gospel message, something he was ignorant of when he was first baptized more than ten years before.

On the first Sunday after his arrival, Dr. Thomas was taken to a Campbellite meeting-house outside of Richmond by a Mr. Malone, whose influence at that meeting helped him secure an invitation to speak that day.

This did not please some in the congregation, for on the following day an accusation was brought forward against Malone for breaking bread with the Doctor and for inviting him to speak at their meeting. Charges were written up to excommunicate Mr. Malone for so grievous an offence, and to excommunicate anyone who would have anything to do with Dr. Thomas. The peculiar thing about all this was Thomas himself had never been excommunicated by any Campbellite church. By this point, he was used to these sort of reactions from those who still saw him as a threat to the unity of Alexander Campbell's reformation efforts.

Though their reaction made little impression upon him, it was nonetheless the catalyst for the commencement of a new ecclesiastical arrangement that resulted in him and a few other brethren regularly meeting on Sundays on what they thought were more Biblical principles than those encountered within the Campbellite churches.

CHAPTER 9

A New Denomination

When great changes occur in history, when great principles
are involved, as a rule the majority are wrong. The minority
are usually right. In every age there have been a few heroic
souls who have been in advance of their time, who have been
misunderstood, maligned, persecuted, sometimes put to
death. [...] This has been true all along the track of the ages.
The men and women who have been in advance, who have
had new ideas, new ideals, who have the courage to attack the
established order of things, have all had to pay the same
penalty.[1]

—EUGENE VICTOR DEBS

I T WAS THROUGH a force of circumstances that Dr. John Thomas
found himself meeting apart from his Campbellite brethren. It was
not his intention to create schism or recruit followers to his name. A
span of five years had passed from the controversy with Alexander
Campbell, and "I was so silent," said the Doctor, "that many of my
friends knew not whether I was dead or alive."[2] Thomas had resisted
fanning the flames of the former controversy and yet the news that he
would occasionally be invited to speak at various Campbellite meeting-
houses was enough to excite murmuring and unrest on the part of others. News concerning Thomas' speaking engagements amongst the
Reformers found its way to Campbell, who in May of 1843 responded
negatively by publishing an article in his *Millennial Harbinger* in which
he brought damaging insinuations against the Doctor's character and
boasted as to how he had humiliated the Doctor several years prior in a
public debate on the topics at the heart of the controversy. Campbell
wrote that the Doctor had at that time made an agreement with him to

---

1. "State of New York—Assembly Chapter," *New York Legislative Documents*, vol. XII,
   no. 35, pt. 2 (Albany: J. B. Lyon Co., 1920), p. 2230–2.
2. John Thomas, *Herald of the Future Age*, vol. 1 (Richmond), p. 86.

abandon his controversial views, which the Doctor strongly and flatly denied.

Campbell's published narrative galled several who were acquainted with the debate, the agreement in question, and with Dr. Thomas' character. Several individuals, along with a Campbellite congregation, wrote to Campbell in an attempt to set the record straight. They spoke highly of the Doctor and charged the editor with injustice and with misrepresenting the facts and character of the Doctor. In a certificate signed by the elder and fifteen others of a Campbellite meeting in Illinois, they informed Campbell:

> We, therefore, without hesitation, pronounce that there is not a vestige of truth in the above extract, which we cannot but regard as a gratuitous calumny upon him. [...] In relation to the Doctor's character, we are happy in being able to rebut the falsehood which would hold it up to reprobation.—There is no man in Kane county, whose character stands fairer; [....][3]

There was a time when Thomas' relationship to the Stone-Campbell Movement was such that he was permitted to publicly speak among many members of the denomination. He had never been disfellowshipped by his home church, and those meeting-places which were opposed to his presence among them were adverse primarily because they had adopted Alexander Campbell's sentiments and believed what Campbell had printed in his *Harbinger* concerning him.

As 1844 passed, Thomas, who by now was accustomed to the animosity shown to him by many within the Restoration Movement, grew less and less sympathetic with a movement which professed to be a return to apostolic simplicity but lacked consistency and earnestness, and which imitated itself after some of the denominational practices which in theory it condemned. As some of the leaders of the Stone-Campbell Movement grew more and more hostile towards the Doctor, despising his manner of plain speech and his use of logic in refuting his antagonists and his calling out the inconsistencies of the movement. It

---

3. Signed by Elder John Oatman, and fifteen others. See "Letter from the Editor to a Friend in the Far West," *Herald of the Future Age*, vol. 1 (1844) (Richmond), p. 64.

was becoming apparent to him that this "reformation movement" was interested in reform only up to a certain point, and no further.

The following extract will help the reader better understand his disappointment and charges against the Stone-Campbell Movement:

> Our object in bringing these things to light is to put such "reformers" to shame; and to let good men see the deception which is practised upon them; when they are called upon by interested partizans to uphold such a system of things under pretence of its being sacred and apostolic! We yearn for such a state of society as will reflect the principles of God's word; where his testimony is the delight and glory of the people. We love the truth too well to allow mankind to be imposed upon with counterfeit metal instead of the pure gold. "This reformation" in Eastern Virginia, is a mere apology for apostolicity. It is sound neither in doctrine nor morality. It began with a show of zeal for truth and liberty, but it has ended in establishing a new form of human authority and tradition.[4]

Stone and Campbell had originally aimed to begin a movement which would unite all Christian sects and denominations by restoring first century Christianity as a basis for such unity. However, as Dr. Thomas eventually discovered, this unification was taking place in the absence of several first century teachings. He felt obligated to not only call out the movement's departure from their aim, but to share with others those missing doctrines which were primarily focused on the kingdom of God—a literal kingdom upon the earth ruled by the Messiah—and the hope of Israel (i.e., the resurrection of the dead), as well as how the popular belief in immortal souls undermined both of these first principles of the Christian faith.

---

4. John Thomas, "Pencillings by the Way," *Herald of the Future Age*, vol. 3, no. 2 (Richmond: 1846), p. 39.

Visit to New York

In October of 1846, Dr. Thomas paid the first of many return visits to New York. These visits were the result of a conversation with a friend who believed that the Doctor's message would receive a warmer welcome in New York than it had in the southern states. His friend was about to visit the region and invited the Doctor to join him. The Doctor accepted the invitation and contrary to his friend's assessment of the place, he found not only the weather but also the region's interest in the Bible rather cold. Upon arrival, Dr. Thomas petitioned for the use of a Disciples of Christ meeting-house, and after an interview, was granted permission. It was here that he gave a series of ten lectures on the future kingdom of God on earth and of God's anointed King for that kingdom: Jesus of Nazareth. And it was here that the differences between himself and the Reformation Movement were crystallized in his mind. He published a Declaration of his faith in an 1847 edition of the *Herald*, within which he explained:

First, then, they [the Scriptures] reveal that THE GOSPEL WAS PREACHED TO ABRAHAM.

This is proved by what follows:—"The Scripture foreseeing that God would justify the Heathen through faith, preached before the Gospel unto Abraham, saying, In thee shall all the Nations be blessed—Gal. iii. 8. Referring to this incident, Jesus said to the Jews, "Your father, Abraham, rejoiced to see my day: and he saw it, and was glad.—John viii. 56.

Upon this we may remark, that all nations have never yet been blessed in Abraham; secondly, that, when all nations shall be blessed in Abraham, Messiah's Day will have been revealed; and thirdly, that these events not having been accomplished, their fulfilment is yet a matter of Hope; hence, Abraham rejoiced in the prospect of the Future Age, then far off, but now near, because it was doubtless then revealed to him that he should sit down with his Descendant, the Messiah, in the Kingdom of God (Luke xiii. 28.); for, Abraham, when called, went out into a country where the Kingdom is to be set up;

which country, "*he should after receive for an inheritance*;" "he sojourned in (this) the Land of Promise, as in a strange, or foreign country; for he looked for a City, or State, which hath foundation, whose builder and maker (or founder and constitutor) is God—Heb. xi. 8–10. […] This was the Ancient Gospel, preached to Abraham, which is still a matter of Hope to all of Abraham's Seed.

Query: Of those who preach [only] "baptism for remission, &c." as the Ancient Gospel,[5] we would inquire—when the gospel was preached to Abraham by the Lord God, did he preach to him, that Jesus was the Christ, His Son; that he died, was buried, and rose again, for faith; and repentance and baptism into the name of the Trinity for the remission of sins, in obedience to that faith? In the nature of things this could not have been preached, yet He preached to him The Gospel; and you admit, that there is but One Gospel: how do you disentangle yourselves from this difficulty? Is it not manifest, that we have been preaching something else than what the Lord God preached to Abraham, and which Paul says was the Gospel?[6] […]

---

5. A reference to the Campbellites.
6. John Thomas was highlighting a point that is overlooked by most, i.e., how *prior to Jesus' crucifixion and resurrection* both Jesus and his disciples had unquestionably preached the gospel message to the citizens of Judea, Galilee and Samaria, and yet the very disciples who preached the gospel before Jesus' death were ignorant of or expressed disbelief in the truths that Jesus had to die, be buried, and rise again, (Matthew 4:23, 9:35, 16:22; Mark 1:14-15, 9:10, 32; Luke 9:6, 45, 16:6, 18:34, 20:1.) From this, Dr. Thomas concluded that the truth and content of the gospel message must consist of *more* than just facts concerning Jesus' existence, his death, burial and resurrection. In his "Declaration," he showed how an essential element of early Christianity was missing from the mainstream "Gospel" of his day, a truth that he felt was essential to saving faith, and which made him so adamant that this missing truth be recognized within the Restoration Movement. That missing truth was the good news of the *kingdom of God*, (Acts 8:12, 19:8, 28:23,31). Dr. Thomas, therefore, felt dutybound to share this truth with the Campbellite churches that would permit him. What resulted from the introduction of these ideas into his preaching, however, was mostly criticism and unrest.

From these texts it is plain, that to preach the gospel was to preach about the Kingdom of God; and *vice versa*, that to preach the Kingdom of God was to preach the Gospel. [...][7]

Philip's discourse consisted of two general divisions; *first*, "the things concerning THE KINGDOM OF GOD;" and *secondly*, concerning "*the* NAME *of Jesus Christ*;"[8]

Thomas' ten lectures in New York stirred a member of the congregation to ask the Doctor if he would be interested in becoming their pastor if the position was to be offered to him. On this he replied:

With many thanks to our brother for his kind disposition, we answer emphatically, "No." We cannot afford to sell our independence for a mess of pottage. How could we faithfully teach the rich the unpalatable doctrine of Christ concerning the proper use of the mammon of unrighteousness, and be dependent upon them for the perishable pittance of a few hundreds per annum? We must be free if we would be faithful to the truth. We object not to receive contributions in aid of the cause we advocate; but they must be *spontaneous*, not extorted. We cannot preach for hire.[9]

---

7. It was on account of this realization that Dr. Thomas could never be reconciled to the teachings of the Restoration Movement, for Alexander Campbell and the churches that were formed out of the Stone-Campbell Movement believed that the visible Church *is itself* the kingdom of God, and that they accordingly held to the belief that this kingdom was established on the day of Pentecost shortly after Jesus' resurrection. Thomas felt that this interpretation was a gross error which essentially left out half of the gospel truth necessary for a proper faith in Jesus and his mission. One outcome of this discovery was that Dr. Thomas repudiated his own baptism by Walter Scott, performed in 1832, and was re-baptized in 1847. The rationale behind his action was that he believed that if a person appreciably changed their mind on doctrines fundamental to salvation, that person should be re-baptized to signify repentance of the old understanding.

8. John Thomas, "Declaration," *Herald of the Future Age*, vol. 3, no. 4 (March 1847) (Richmond), pp. 76, 79.

9. Robert Roberts, *Dr. Thomas: His Life and Work* (Birmingham: C. C. Walker, 1911), p. 200.

European Tour

In May of 1848, Dr. Thomas left his home in Virginia with the plan to set sail for Europe, via New York, hoping to lay the truths of the gospel of the kingdom of God before a new audience. Upon revisiting New York, he was permitted by two Campbellite congregations to speak on this and related topics in their places of meeting. The hope was that a similar reception would be found on the other side of the Atlantic. However, once he arrived in his native country, he discovered that his reputation has preceded him, and unlike many of the meeting-houses in America, those of Campbellite persuasion in Britain were mostly closed to him. Reformation periodicals in America and England had admonished their churches to refuse the Doctor a venue to speak once it was learned that he had plans to sail to Europe. But not every door was closed. A Campbellite periodical published in London, the *Gospel Banner*, was willing to give him the benefit of the doubt and it provided him with an outlet for his message, as did at least one Millerite congregation.[10]

Among those British Campbellite congregations that agreed to give the Doctor a platform to speak, ruptures would sometimes occur when members aligned themselves with his position. In Nottingham, he was able to speak thirteen times, gaining newspaper coverage and favorable reviews. Out of this, a small community was formed which began meeting on a regular basis. In Glasgow, the interest in his lectures forced him to make use of City Hall which was able to seat up to six thousand people. On the last night, many of the multitude could not obtain admission, after which a soirée was held in the Doctor's honor. It had been his intention to return to America shortly after his lectures in Glasgow had concluded, however, many of the attendees at the soirée complained that he was leaving their fair land all too swiftly, and asked if was possible for him to defer his return and in the interim to publish in book form the subject of his lectures?

He obliged their request and for the remainder of 1848, and into the next year, worked on the publication of *Elpis Israel: An Exposition of*

---

10. The Millerites were a Christian sect who followed the prophetic teachings of preacher William Miller, who calculated that the return of Jesus would be on October 22, 1844.

the Kingdom of God.[11] One chapter in this book was devoted to the restoration of the Jewish race to the land of Israel, which he determined must soon take place in accord with Ezekiel chapters 36-39, and of which he wrote about in detail. The following is a sample of his thoughts on the topic:

> There is, then, a partial and primary restoration of the Jews before the advent of Christ, which is to serve as the nucleus, or basis, of future operations in the restoration of the rest of the tribes after he has appeared in the kingdom. The pre-advental colonization of Palestine will be on purely political principles; and the Jewish colonists will return in unbelief of the Messiaship [sic] of Jesus, and of the truth as it is in him. They will emigrate thither as agriculturists and traders in the hope of ultimately establishing their commonwealth, but more immediately of getting rich in silver and gold by commerce with India, and in cattle and goods by their industry at home under the efficient protection of the British power. [...]

> I know not whether the men, who at present contrive the foreign policy of Britain, entertain the idea of assuming the sovereignty of the Holy Land, and of promoting its colonization by the Jews; their present intentions, however, are of no importance one way or the other; because they will be compelled, by events soon to happen, to do what, under existing circumstances, heaven and earth combined could not move them to attempt. The present decisions of "statesmen" are destitute of stability. A shooting star in the political firmament is sufficient to disturb all the forces of their system; and to stultify all the theories of their political astronomy. The finger of God has indicated a course to be pursued by Britain which cannot be evaded, and which her counsellors will not only be willing, but eager, to adopt when the crisis comes upon them.[12]

---

11. *Elpis Israel* is Greek for "the hope of Israel."
12. John Thomas, *Elpis Israel* (London: 1849), pp. 395-6.

These words of Dr. Thomas were written nearly 30 years before the publication of Theodore Herzl's *The State of the Jews* and the meeting of the First Zionist Congress. They were also written some 70 years before the signing of the Balfour Declaration which announced Britain's support for the establishment of a "national home for the Jewish people" in Palestine, and a full century before Israel became a sovereign nation in their own homeland after the British pulled out of Palestine in 1948. And lastly, these words of Dr. Thomas were also some of the "speculations" that Alexander Campbell and others in the Restoration Movement condemned him for teaching.

After *Elpis Israel* was published, and after a tour of 1700 miles through Holland, Prussia, Germany, Belgium, France and Great Britain, Dr. Thomas returned to the U.S. in late 1850 after an absence of more than two years.

Upon docking in New York, the Doctor was invited to speak on the kingdom of God at both Campbellite and non-Campbellite venues before he eventually returned home to Virginia.

Home Again

After his return from Europe, Dr. Thomas, for the most part, spent his time lecturing and writing on Bible subjects. He traveled up and down the continent, visiting both Canada (including Nova Scotia, Windsor, Halifax, Toronto) and various states within the U.S. (upper East Coast, Ohio, Kentucky, Mississippi, Tennessee, Iowa). One of the highlights of his efforts included a three night lecture series held at the Hall of Delegates belonging to the Virginia House of Delegates, an event that was officially granted by that legislative body of the Commonwealth of Virginia.

In 1852, he announced his plan to relocate from Richmond to the greater region of New York City. One of the reasons given was the latter's size, being more than fifteen times larger than the capital of Virginia, which presented an opportunity to share the gospel of the kingdom of God to a potentially larger audience. One of the benefits of moving to Greater New York was the ability to rent the grand and spacious Chelsea Hall, where weekly breaking of bread services and Bible lectures were

conducted and which interestingly would a few years later become a
focal point of Jewish life.

From 1858 to 1861, in addition to editing the monthly *Herald*,
Thomas worked on the publication of additional books, including *Ana-
tolia*, which was an exposition of prophecy, detailing the inevitable fall
of the French and Ottoman (Turkish) Empires, and the ascendancy of
the Russian nation, and a 3-volume exposition of the book of Revelation, titled *Eureka*.

By the time the first volume of *Eureka* was published, it was clear
that the U.S. political climate was in turmoil and things looked to be getting dangerously worse. The controversy was between the northern
states, which were primarily given to manufacturing, and the southern
states, which were almost entirely agricultural and dependent upon
slave labor. The two sections of the country were bitterly divided on the
question of slavery. In April 1861, the simmering troubles erupted into
full-scale war when a new constitution was adopted by a convention of
southern states which voted unanimously to secede from the former
union of states under the new title, "The Confederate States of America."

Civil War and Failed Aspirations

Shortly after war broke out between the two sides, postal commu-
nications were interrupted, making it difficult to communicate with
those living in the South.[13] Despite the dangers and constraints on pub-
licizing his visits ahead of time, Dr. Thomas nonetheless decided to
embark on a tour through the southern territories which were once a
part of his home and where many of his friends still lived. And so in
June of 1861, he set off on his journey into the war zone.

Accompanying him were letters of introduction, written by friends
who were now in the Confederate Army, including ones from a colonel
and a general, which requested that Dr. Thomas be given safe passage
wherever he traveled. While visiting Tennessee and Kentucky, it came
into his mind to visit Richmond, which was now the capital of the Confederacy and one of the primary targets of the war. He arrived in

---

13. These circumstances forced Dr. Thomas to eventually cease publication of the
    monthly *Herald*.

Richmond by railway under conditions difficult and tedious, and found the city a campground for the Confederate armies. The Doctor recorded the details of this visit in the *Herald*:

> Having arrived in the capital of Virginia, and of "the Confederate States of America" for the time being, we reported ourselves at what became our headquarters while sojourning in the New Dominion. These were the very hospitable quarters of our friend and brother Dr. F. Davison on Maine street, Richmond. We were received with surprise and a hearty welcome, being the least expected of any of his acquaintants; for there had been no means of communicating our intention of visiting the state in this its hour of peril.
>
> It was soon known to the brethren that we were with them; and it was not long before it was arranged that the southern public was to be addressed by one from the northern state of New Jersey. A notice was therefore inserted in the *Daily Dispatch* inviting the citizens of Richmond to hear us at Bethel, a meeting-house belonging to the brethren, on Sunday morning; and at the Corinthian Hall on Maine street, in the afternoon; and on three nights in the week. The weather being very

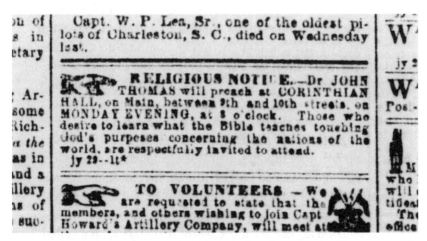

Advertisement in the *Richmond Daily Dispatch* for July 29, 1861 announcing public lectures to be given by John Thomas—lectures which were held in the thick of the American Civil War.

hot, and the hall badly ventilated, and the war attracting all things to itself, the attendance was much less than at our former visit; especially in the week, when but for the presence of some of the brethren, there would have been scarcely any audience at all.

On Sunday afternoon, which was the most numerous meeting, we addressed the people on the great national crisis brought upon the country in the providence of God. [...]

We concluded our address by advising our brethren to have nothing to do with the factions on either side. Both sides proclaim to the world that God is with them, and each is repudiating the other as the greatest sinners under and against heaven. In this mutual accusation there is more truth than fiction. All the States and their peoples are guilty, and all under condemnation—"there is none of them righteous, no, not one." The South says, it is fighting for "a pure christianity" against the infidels of the North! The Northern abolitionists, and all other classes, are infidel enough. Every one intelligent in the word knows this. But this blackness and darkness does not whiten and illumine the South. There is no pure christianity in North or South, apart from the belief of "the gospel of the kingdom," and the obedience it demands; and where in either section are they to be found who will stand this test of purity? Not the Puritans, or rather, Simon Pures, of New England, nor the Sectarians, whose faith and practice is common to North and South. If to be found at all, they are only with the few so microscopic in its dimensions as almost to elude detection. Hence christians of the bible order can take no part with either, and be guiltless before God. If Southern and Northern Methodists, Baptists, Campbellites, Presbyterians, Episcopalians, and Papists, think fit to blow one another's brains out, and so send their brethren to hell and the Devil according to their creeds, by all means let them do it to their hearts' content; but let not christians mingle in the unhallowed strife.[14]

The reference to Campbellites blowing "one another's brains outs" would have struck a nerve within the Restoration Movement, for the "fathers" of that movement were staunchly anti-war on Christian principle, and had from time to time emphasized on the pages of their periodicals the incongruity of Christian soldiers killing one another. However, the churches that associated themselves with Campbell and Stone never made this position a test of fellowship, so when war broke out in 1861 there was little to constrain Campbellites on both sides of the conflict from, as the Doctor put it, "sending their brethren to hell"[15] on the battlefield.

It was little more than a decade before the Civil War that in 1848 Alexander Campbell had delivered a two-hour-long "Address on War," which strongly condemned all Christian participation in war. Analyzing 286 wars from the time of Constantine the Great until the Mexican War, Campbell argued that not one of them was for defense alone. Most were for plunder, forced tribute, extension of territory, retaliation, civil wars, contested titles to crowns, religious wars, or disputes over boundaries. Campbell laid much of the blame upon the priests and ministers of God, and said that the pulpit had become the handmaid of war:

> Sabbath after Sabbath, for years and years, have the pulpits on one side of a sea or river, and those on the other side, resounded with prayers for the success of rival armies, as if God could hear them both, and make each triumphant over the other, guiding and commissioning swords and bullets to the heads and hearts of their respective enemies![16]

He concluded, "Need we any other proof that a Christian people can, in no way whatever, countenance a war as a proper means of redressing wrongs, of deciding justice, or of settling controversies among nations?"

---

14. John Thomas, *Herald of the Kingdom and Age to Come*, Oct. 1861 (West Hoboken), pp. 226–240.
15. In the theology of Dr. Thomas and the Christadelphians, "hell" would have been a reference to the dominion of the grave (i.e., the death state).
16. Alexander Campbell, "An Address on War," *Millennial Harbinger*, 1848, p. 377.

Barton Stone, the other half of the Stone-Campbell Movement, like Campbell, rejected the notion that Christ's disciples were permitted to fight in the wars of men:

> Nothing appears so repugnant to the kingdom of heaven as war—Christians, who love as brethren, fighting against Christians with deadly hate! Christians whose duty and work is to save the world, fighting against the wicked, and hurrying them unprepared into eternal punishment. Is this to love our neigbor [sic] as our selves?[17]

Campbell and Stone were not alone in teaching that non-violence was an essential element in the movement's objective of returning to the original order of the first-century Church. One of the most influential of the pre-Civil War Campbellite leaders was William Kimbrough Pendleton, who by the outbreak of the War had taken over from Campbell the duties of publishing the movement's mouthpiece, *The Millennial Harbinger*. Shortly after the outbreak of fighting between Union and Confederate troops in 1861, Pendleton published "A Plea for Peace," exhorting Christians to abstain from the cruel spectacle of fighting:

> O, my christian brother, think of it! When you shoulder your musket and equip yourself with all the instruments of death, ask yourself have you the right thus to take the life of your fellow? who gave you the right? what has your brother done that you may shoot him?—Has he stolen your property? can you murder him for that! Has he differed with you about political governments? can you not part in peace?... Let not brother meet brother in battle. Let not two christian souls perishing by mutual violence, going down to death, frantic with the rage of mortal combat, hope to rise to the climes of celestial peace from such a struggle! There is a nobler work for the the [sic] people of God.[18]

---

17. "Civil and Military Offices Sought and Held by Christians," *Christian Messenger*, May 1842, p. 205. Stone also wrote in 1844: "A nation professing christianity, yet teaching, learning and practicing the arts of war, cannot be the kingdom of Christ, nor do they live in obedience to the laws of Christ—the government is anti-christian, and must reap the fruits of their infidelity at some future day."

Yet the plea fell mostly on deaf ears. Though it was taught from the pulpit and the printed page for decades, albeit irregularly, the problem was that the matter of conscientious objection to war was not made a test of fellowship within the three most populous denominations that grew out of the Stone-Campbell Movement.[19] Consequently, each member of these churches was free to form their own opinion on the matter. The result of such freedom, and irregular emphasis on the topic, became even more evident as time passed. As the movement's membership swelled, an awareness of the founders' views that Christians should not participate in warfare was not passed on, and consequently these churches began to mirror the culture of an ever increasingly interventionist and militaristic America. By World War I, many of its members had come to see the non-violent views of its pioneers as an embarrassment. After World War I, those in mainstream Churches of Christ moved toward a pro-war stance.[20] According to Hughes: "One observes among Churches of Christ from that date [August 1917] forward a gradual disintegration of the pacifist sentiment until, by the early 1960's, pacifism had almost entirely vanished from this fellowship."[21] Pearl Harbor effectively ended the promotion of pacifist ideals within the denomination. The patriotism of the post-World War II era and the rise of the threat of Communism shifted the denomination even further away from their earlier non-violent beliefs. Patriotism had now become equated with Christianity and true piety.

Though small pockets of conscientious objectors still exist today, for the most part the descendants of the Stone-Campbell Movement have dismissed Christian non-violence in the face of war as naïve and impractical: a teaching left over from the forgotten past, inscribed in a few dusty magazines of yesteryear. Today, most in the remnants of this movement view pacifism as an idea utterly foreign to the American perspective of God and country and would be surprised to learn of their

---

18. *Millennial Harbinger*, July 1861, pp. 409–10.
19. These three were the Churches of Christ, the Christian Church and the Disciples of Christ.
20. Douglas A. Foster, Paul M. Blowers, Anthony L. Dunnavant, and D. Newell Williams, *The Encyclopedia of the Stone-Campbell Movement*, (Grand Rapids: Eerdmans, 2005), p. 587.
21. Richard T. Hughes, "The Apocalyptic Origins of Churches of Christ and the Triumph of Modernism," *Religion and American Culture* 2(2) (1992), p. 201.

early leaders' support of it. These Restorationist churches have been assimilated into the American mainstream church view, exchanging non-violence for patriotism. But in 1861, the pacifist teachings of its founders weren't foreign, they were just simply ignored by the Campbellites who enlisted to fight and kill their neighbors and brethren on the battlefield. When it came to the matter of war, the movement failed to live up to the aspirations of its founders. This was just one more example of what Dr. Thomas saw as a failure of the Restoration Movement.

Dr. Thomas could see the divorce between doctrine and moral practice within the Movement, and it was something that he would not forget as Christian bonds during the war began to unravel. To him, it was unthinkable that any Christian denomination could fail to make this matter a test of fellowship. He considered conscientious objection to war as one of the pillars upon which all Christian churches should be upheld.[22] And so, on the first day of his public lectures, he concluded:

> There is no government or country on earth, apart from Jehovah's land, that is worthy the blood of one of his saints. Let the potsherds of the earth fight for their own governments, in scripture styled *"the Devil and his Angels;"* the time of the saints is not yet quite come. All they have to do now is to pray for *"all in authority,"* without regard to latitude, longitude, or generation; not that they may be converted, but that their policy may be so providentially overruled as that they may be permitted to "lead quiet and peaceable lives in all godliness and honesty." [...]

> Such in substance was our discourse in the Confederate Capital. No one put us to the question on account of it, nor are we aware that there was any disposition to interrupt us as dangerous to the "powers that be."[23]

---

22. As one Campbellite historian described it, "John Thomas and his faction within the Campbell Movement held to a dogmatic pacifism. They were the only pre-Civil War division within the movement, and embraced a very strong and specific pacifism." (Jim Cook, *The Myth of the Stone-Campbell Movement* (Lanham: Lexington Books, 2019), p. 120.)

23. John Thomas, *Herald of the Kingdom and Age to Come*, Oct. 1861 (West Hoboken), pp. 226–40.

Though he recorded that the "powers that be" had kept their peace that Sunday during his lecture, this state of affairs would not last for long.

The Powers That Be

After his lectures were completed in the Confederate capital, Dr. Thomas visited a small meeting-place some 80 miles to the southwest, arriving there on Saturday, August 9th. In his journal, he documented what happened upon his arrival:

> As is usual there, the congregations are always considerable, the brethren themselves making quite a respectable assembly. We were gratified to see them once more, though not so much on hearing that the war fever had disturbed the temperature of some of them. From what we had heard we judged that it would be wholesome to "put them in remembrance" of the necessity of walking in the truth, as well as of getting into Christ, if they would attain to his kingdom and glory. If they were possessed with the spirit of war, and made war speeches to ignorant multitudes to stir up their ungodly lusts to hate their enemies and take vengeance of them, what difference was there between their spirit and that of the world? As Christians we must not mingle in the strife, but be quiet come what will; and if the contending parties will not let us alone, then clear out from under their dominion. The saints had nothing to do with patriotism, or zeal for the country of one's birth or adoption. Christ who is the Elder Brother and the First Born of the Divine Family, *"left them an example that they should walk in his steps"*—1 Pet. ii, 21. He was no patriot, nor did he inculcate patriotism, according to the flesh. He wept over the faithlessness and disobedience of Jerusalem, the future throne of his dominion; but he neither fought for it, nor exhorted his countrymen to do so, in view of the invasion of Judea, and the destruction of the city and temple by the Romans. On the contrary, he sent his armies against it, and told his friends in Judea to flee to the mountains, and those in the midst of it to

emigrate, and those in the countries of the Gentiles not to
enter it; for that those who neglected his warning should fall
by the sword, and be led away into slavery among all nations.
The saints who are really such, have no zeal nor enthusiasm
for anything but the truth and its interests. Their country is
the land promised to Abraham and his seed; and the commonwealth of their adoption, Israel's, it the Day of Christ.
Instead of the Star Spangled Banner or the Confederate Flag,
their's is the ensign of Judah's Lion to be planted on Zion when
the dominion shall come to her. Isa. v, 26; xi, 10, 12; xviii, 3;
xlix, 22; lix, 19; lxii, 10; Mic. iv, 7, 8. This is the banner that
exhausts all our patriotism. The Royal Standard of the Kingdom whose ample folds will be unfurled by the Majesty of the
Heavens, when he shall invade the peoples with his troops.
Hab. iii 3–16.[24]

After the reaquaintances were completed that day, the Doctor
retired for the evening not far from the meeting-house, but not without
first securing a speaking appointment for the next day before the Sunday congregation. But local law enforcement had other plans:

When we arrived we found a large collection of people; and
the first who welcomed us was bro. Hamlin, who had that
morning ridden twenty miles to meeting. The greeting past,
he drew us aside and informed us that the police were on the
ground, and had come to prevent our speaking and to put us
under arrest. While imparting this ominous information,
brother Joel Ragsdale, a former magistrate of the county, presented himself with a newspaper in his hand, and inviting us
to follow him apart, asked us if we had seen a certain "Act of
the Confederate Congress" published in Friday's Dispatch? We
had. "Well," said he, "the police are here, to arrest you under its
provisions. There are two of them, and both Methodists, and
have been set on by their brethren; who, two months ago
threatened that if you came here in these troublous times, they
would have you arrested. They asked me if you were a citizen

---

24. Thomas, ibid.

of the United States, and I told them I thought you were; and it is against these that the Act is most especially levelled." That we perceive, but they will find that they have missed the mark. Where are the men? Let us go to them.

Crossing the open space toward the officers of the law, the crowd, which had much of it collected to see what was going to happen, followed and surrounded the parties in the case. Bro. Ragsdale introduced us to the officers, one of whom was named Garland, and the other Coleman. The former a good natured looking man, and did all the talking on the police side; while the other had a dark and malevolent expression undisturbed by a smiling feature, when all around were laughing. He uttered but one sentence all the time, and that in a gruff and hollow tone, ordering the other to "*make the arrest!*"

Having introduced us, and the ceremony of hand-shaking being over, bro. Ragsdale proceeded to make some remarks, but ended suddenly by observing to them, "but the doctor will state his own case." As we had no case before us to state, we remarked to the police that we must first know of them what they wanted with us? Officer Garland asked us if we had seen "the Act respecting Alien Enemies?" We said we had; and, acting upon the hint in Paul's case, who though "a Hebrew of the Hebrews," fell back in a certain extremity upon his Roman citizenship, we claimed that being an Englishman, the act could not be applied to us. That as such we were an alien friend, and not an alien enemy; for that England was not at war with the Confederate States, though the federalists were. They did not ask us if we were a citizen of the United States. We pressed upon their attention that we were an Englishman, which they did not dispute; but still seemed to think that we were a dangerous Englishman and ought not to be at large. We inquired, for what did they wish to arrest us? We had been preaching doctrine dangerous to the government. How? In saying that people should not bear arms. We told them that was a mistake. Our proposition was that *Christians* should not fight; and that if they arrested us for that, they ought to arrest all our brethren in the country; for if they did not say so, yet if faithful to the truth, they ought to hold it. Now, we continued, Christians in our sense of the word, which is the scriptural sense, are *they who have intelligently believed the gospel of the kingdom, and subsequently obeyed it in immersion.* These are they, called "saints," whom we believe to be interdicted [sic] the use of deadly weapons against men until Christ comes. We do not say that Methodists, Presbyterians, Baptists, and such like, should not bear arms. Of these, we say, carry as many arms as you please; blow out one another's brains to your hearts' content, and when you are exhausted you will cease. It is all the same whether they die thus, or in their beds; not being Christians they are a law to themselves, and heirs of capture and destruction every way.

But they considered that if our doctrine prevailed the country would be overrun by the invader. We urged that they need not be afraid of that, for very few would believe it. Nor was such a result apprehended by those who wished our arrest. It was a mere sectarian pretence to gratify private personal malevolence. Upon this officer Garland said, he did not wish to lend himself to such influence; and that he had proposed that three county magistrates be chosen to hear the case who belonged to no sect; which we afterward learned would be impossible to find. Judging from his countenance, which had an honest sort of expression, we did not suppose he did; but this was more than we could suppose of all in these parts; for there were those among them who had said, they would like to see us hanged, and might imagine that the times were favorable for that result.

But, taking out our watch, we remarked, what you do, do quickly. It is a matter of perfect indifference to us whether you arrest us or not; but if you wish to avoid trouble, we should advise you not to burden yourself with us. It may be fortunate for us if you do; for we shall then be on Mr. Jeff. Davis' hands; and he will have the trouble and expense of sending us out of the country, which would be no little convenience to us, as, otherwise, we may have to return north by the long and costly route through Kentucky. This raised a laugh which was no prejudice to our affairs. What shall we do? said officer Garland to his colleague. "Make the arrest!" was the ominous response. Well, gentlemen, be quick; our appointment was for eleven o'clock, and it is now twenty minutes past. We have come to speak and the people to hear us, and if you do not arrest, we must begin. We paused for their action. But they seemed not to know what to do. We then remarked that time was precious, and as they had not made up their minds, we would say, that we should pass the night at Mr. Ragsdale's whom they all knew; and that if they concluded to arrest, they would find us there. They said, "they would take counsel," which we were informed, they did. A lawyer on the ground whom they consulted told them they could do nothing with us. But of this they were not satisfied, and said they would take further counsel on the morrow, which was court day. We heard that they did, but the advice did not strengthen them, and they did not venture to "make the arrest." Having told them where to find us, we left them to their reflections, and proceeded to the house which was full to overflowing. The police, we were told, did not come in. Perhaps they had heard enough from us outside, where they had come to grief, being foiled in their purpose, and a jest before the people.[25]

Dr. Thomas was able to complete his exhortation in peace that day, and after a few stops later that summer in Charlottesville, Richmond, and Norfolk, was able to ultimately find safe passage back to New Jersey from where he had originated some three months prior.

With his work in America being hampered by the war, he was encouraged to revisit Britain, which he did, arriving in May 1862. He then set out on an arduous lecturing tour, completing his speaking duties that winter. Before returning to America, it was decided to begin a new religious periodical to replace the *Herald*, which had been suspended on account of the war. The new magazine would be titled *The*

---

25. Thomas, ibid.

Ambassador of the Coming Age, and edited by a 23-year old newspaper reporter, Robert Roberts.

In February of 1863, Thomas returned to America where he resumed his usual activities, writing occasional letters and articles that appeared in the new *Ambassador*, as well as lecturing and working on the third volume of *Eureka*.

The Most Extraordinary Church

In 1864, while America's Civil War was still being fought, Dr. Thomas chose to embark on a 3000-mile tour of Canada and the U.S. In July of that year, he arrived at Henderson, Kentucky, which at the time was regarded by the Federal authorities as within "the rebel lines." It was during his visit there that the Confederate Military Commander issued a proclamation that all male citizens aged 17–45 should report themselves to his headquarters before August 15th to show cause why they should not be conscripted into the army of the Confederacy. The following account appeared in *The Ambassador* recounting the chosen course of action:

> The proclamation very much disturbed the minds of the brethren, for there were 10 of them liable to conscription. I told them that I thought they might get clear, and that if they would authorize me to go to the rebel headquarters, and depute one of their number to accompany me, I did not doubt, if there were any regard for law and scripture, that the evil might be averted. The Confederate law exempts all "Ministers of the Gospel" from rendering military service to the state, and by proving that they were ministers of the gospel, they might find exemption under that law. But how was that to be done? Easily enough. The apostle Peter in writing to christians without distinction dispersed throughout Pontus, Galatia, Cappadocia, Asia and Bithynia, whom he styles "elect" or chosen ones "through sanctification of spirit unto obedience and sprinkling of Jesus Christ's blood." To these obedient and blood-sprinkled believers, he says, "Ye are a holy priesthood." For what are they a holy priesthood? "To offer up spiritual

sacrifices acceptable to the Deity through Jesus Christ." [...] It is true the lawmakers knew nothing about all this when they legislated for the exemption of "ministers of the gospel." Their ignorance does not invalidate our rights; it only confers upon others who are not ministers of the gospel a share in what really exclusively belongs to us, who are Brethren in Christ. They understood this, and were quite willing that the experiment should be made, but not, I think, very sanguine of its success.[26]

When Dr. Thomas and his companions arrived at the camp they requested an interview with the recruiting officer, Colonel Napier:

[...] we inquired which of the persons around us was Col. Napier? We were directed to a middle aged unwarlike looking gentleman in his shirt sleeves, or rather, in a violet colored flannel shirt, without hat, cap, or coat, standing by a felled oak upon which rested the leaf of a table, which in fair weather, served for the Official desk, where all Red-Tape affairs were disposed of without circumlocution. We bowed a mutual recognition, upon which brother Stone rather incautiously, as I thought, introduced me as "Dr. Thomas of New York!" The Colonel gave a start of surprise, and then looking steadily in my face, said "What! from New York? Why doctor aint you afraid to come among us?" I replied "no sir, I have been among the Confederates before. I spent some hours with my friend Gen. Magruder at Yorktown, who sent me with an escort through his lines as a present to General Wood at Fortress Monroe. I live indeed in New Jersey, but I belong to neither North nor South." "Well," said he, "we do not make war upon women and children, and unarmed citizens." "It would be well, sir;" I replied, if both parties would observe the same rule." "Yes," said he, "it would."

---

26. John Thomas, "Tour in the United States and Canada—Letter from Dr Thomas," *Ambassador of the Coming Age*, vol. 1, no. 6 (December 1864), p. 89.

We then introduced our business to him, telling him that we were a deputation from certain persons in Henderson Co., who claimed exemption from military service on the ground of being ministers of the gospel, and opposed conscientiously to bearing arms. "Yes," said he, "by the Confederate law all ministers of the gospel are exempt." "We have certificates duly authenticated before a magistrate that the ten persons for whom we appear are ministers of the gospel." "Have they," said he, "each a congregation of his own, and does each of them receive a regular salary?" "No sir, they all belong to one church." "What," he exclaimed, "ten ministers of the gospel in one church; that's the most extraordinary church I ever heard of!" "It is colonel, and the only one of the sort we know of in all Kentucky. But they are *bona fide* ministers of the gospel to all who will hear them, and to administer ordinances." "Well," said he, in a manifest quandary, "it is a singular church. Why all Henderson County might claim exemption by joining your church." "Not so easy, colonel; it is very difficult to join it, because it requires intelligence in the scriptures, and a crucifixion of the affections and lusts."[27]

At first, the colonel refused to grant exemption, but perceiving their determination, decided that in view of an approaching thunderstorm it would be better to grant the Doctor and his companions their request. With the certificates duly endorsed by the adjutant, the appellants fled from the camp, drenched by the torrential rain, driving hard in their one horse buggy all night, in order to reach safety before the authorities could revoke their decision.

The Christadelphians

From Henderson, Kentucky, Dr. Thomas headed for Chicago, and then west to Freeport, Illinois. In so doing, he was leaving Confederate controlled territory and entering the Federal North. While in Freeport

---

27. Thomas, ibid., pp. 90–1.

he stayed with a Bro. Coffman, and was able to meet a few of the brethren from the neighboring towns:

> Next day, I arrived in Freeport, Stephenson Co., Illinois; and
> the day after was conveyed by Mr. Newcomer to bro. S. W.
> Coffman's in Ogle Co. I staid several days in these parts,
> speaking to the people in public and private. I arrived among
> them as one desired. "I am more glad to see you," said bro.
> Coffman, "than I expect you are to see me." They were dis-
> turbed in mind about the coming draft on Sept. 19.; and were
> longing for my arrival in hope that I might be able to help
> them against the Federal provost marshals. I told them that
> the Federal law exempted all who belonged to a Denomina-
> tion conscientiously opposed to bearing arms on condition of
> paying 300 dollars, finding a substitute, or serving in the hos-
> pitals. This excluded all the known denominations except the
> Quakers; for besides this denomination, they not only pro-
> claimed the fighting for country a christian virtue; but were all
> commingled in the unhallowed and sanguinary conflict.
> There was, however, a Denomination not known to the igno-
> rance of legislative wisdom. It was relatively very small, but
> nevertheless a Denomination and a Name, contrary to, and
> distinct from, all others upon earth. It comprehended all those
> who with Paul repudiated the use of carnal weapons; and not
> this only, but who, believing the gospel of the kingdom,
> became constituents of the name by being intelligently
> immersed into Christ Jesus their Lord. The members of this
> name and denomination are not politicians; they are not patri-
> ots, and take no part in the contentions of the world, which is
> "the Enemy of God." Politicians, patriots, and factionists,
> though they may profess the theory of the truth, and have
> passed through the water, have not the spirit of the truth, in
> them, and have therefore, no scriptural claim or identity with
> the conscience of this Name and Denomination. This was
> their view of the matter, and met the case of these brethren in
> Ogle Co., who have a mortal distaste for all crotchets and
> compromise, and refuse all identification with those who
> favor them. Their determination is to be shot at their own

doors, rather than serve in the armies of the North and South; which to them is a degradation and defilement not to be endured by the faithful. Though these are their sentiments they feared that in the browbeating presence of a provost marshall's court, they might not be able to make them stand successfully against the taunts and ridicule that were sure to be brought upon them. They wished therefore that I would write something that they could put into court as the ground of their claim to exemption according to the law. It would be necessary to give the Name a denominational appellative, that being so denominated, they might have wherewith to answer the Inquisitors. This seemed the most difficult part of the affair, though not altogether insurmountable. The crisis had come, and something had to be done to save brethren in deed and in truth from being seized upon by the Devil and Satan; and hurled into the Bottomless Abyss, now engulping with the voraciousness of Death and Hades, the sinners of this ungodly nation. I did not know a better denomination that would be given to such a class of believers than "Brethren in Christ." This declares that true status; and, as officials prefer words to phrases, the same fact is expressed in another form by the word Christadelphians, or Χριστου αδελφοι Christ's Brethren. This matter settled to their satisfaction, I wrote for them the following certificate:—

"This is to certify, that S. W. Coffman (the names of the ten male members in full here) and others constitute a Religious Association denominated herein for the sake of distinguishing them from all other "Names and Denominations," Brethren in Christ, or in one word, Christadelphians; and that said brethren are in fellowship with similar associations in England, Scotland, the British Provinces, New York and other cities of the North and South—New York being for the time present the Radiating Centre of their testimony to the people of the current age and generation of the world.

"This is also to certify, that the Denomination constituted of the associations or ecclesias of this Name, conscientiously opposes, and earnestly protests against "Brethren in Christ" having anything to do with politics in wordy strife, or arms-bearing in the service of the Sin-powers of the world under any conceivable circumstances or conditions whatever; regarding it as a course of conduct disloyal to the Deity in Christ, their Lord and King, and perilous to their eternal welfare.

"This being individually and collectively the conscientious conviction of all true Christadelphians, they claim and demand the rights and privileges so considerately accorded by the Congress of the United States in the statute made and provided for the exemption of members of a Denomination conscientiously opposed to bearing arms in the service of any human government.

"This is also further to certify that the undersigned is the personal instrumentality by which the Christian Association aforesaid in Britain and America have been developed within the last fifteen years, and that therefore he knows assuredly that a conscientious, determined, and uncompromising opposition to serving in the armies of "the Powers that be" is their denominational characteristic.

"JOHN THOMAS."[28]

This certificate was then taken before a notary public, and to it were added the signatures of the Doctor and the applicants. The county seal was then affixed and the document handed to S. W. Coffman for safe keeping until an emergency should arise demanding its production to confound the adversaries. And with this, a new denomination had been born. A new *denomination*—not a cult.

---

28. John Thomas, ibid., vol. 1, no. 7 (January 1865), pp. 105–6.

CHAPTER 10

A Brief Conclusion

I persecuted this Way to the death, binding and
delivering to prison both men and women, as the
high priest and the whole council of elders bear me
witness.

—ACTS 22:4-5, RSV

True penance consists in regretting without ceasing
the faults of the past, and in firmly resolving to
never again commit that which is so deplorable.

—BERNARD OF CLAIRVAUX

DESPITE WHAT THEIR adversaries claim, the Christadelphians fall outside of the spectrum of a cult. They do not
match any of the twenty-three characteristics of a cult as item-
ized and reviewed in chapter 2. Moreover, the positions that they take
on the matters of conditional immortality and the identity of Jesus and
the nature of God—the areas where they are most often attacked—
though they are unorthodox, such positions do not qualify as being
unscriptural. Unless one wishes to label Martin Luther and William
Tyndale as cultists on account of their views on the intermediate state,
and unless one classifies first century Jewish Christians as belonging to a
cult because they did not stray into metaphysical and philosophical
speculations regarding a triadic unity of co-equal "persons" in one
divine "essence," one has to recognize that the Christadelphians are not
much different than these and therefore do not deserve the pejorative
label "cult."

In the opening chapter I shared a personal story of how in 1985,
when I first began my research on the Christadelphians, I visited the
Library of Congress in Washington, DC—the first visit of many. It was
there that a librarian corrected me as I embarked on what I had hoped
would be a simple task of digging up dirt on this little-known group

called the Christadelphians. Her words to me were, "Sir, the Christadelphians are not a cult. They're a sect." This was the first of many instances where I had to accept correction from others. What eventually emerged from my study of the Christadelphians was the realization that I was too quick to judge others.

One other thing that I have learned as a result of this investigation is that we humans—and in particular Christians—are not open to the possibility of being wrong. Too many of us hold our religious beliefs within a clenched fist, unwilling and therefore unable to see possible errors in our respective beliefs. But if Christians are genuine followers of Jesus, then as truth seekers we should not be afraid of allowing our beliefs to be challenged. If our beliefs are well founded, they will be reinforced and strengthened when tested. Conversely, if we engage with those who disagree with us and as a result our beliefs are shown to be weak and flawed, we should be thankful to finally see the errors in our own thinking, freeing us to search anew for what is true and of God.

A third conclusion that I have arrived at, which should come as no surprise, is that the Christadelphians are not perfect. Despite their dedication to pursuing the truth of the Bible and desiring to follow Jesus, they are not without flaws. After all, they are human. Personality conflicts and debates within local ecclesias, as in all churches, can cause divisions, though they are infrequent.

One other criticism that could be brought forward has to do with this denomination's decentralized structure and independent spirit. Because the Christadelphians are a lay organization that eschews salaried pastors, the democratized equality of all of its members can produce a mediocrity in leadership that stifles progress and growth. One may label this the "too many chefs in the kitchen" syndrome, where too many "brothers" are allowed for the sake of fairness and equality to teach and lead within the local ecclesia, even if they are not particularly gifted in those roles. Although there are benefits that result from the sharing of responsibilities within the body, the trade-off is that often the quality of the final product suffers. Because of the fear that a gifted brother might exert too much influence on the body, few are given the freedom to shine to their full potential. On the one hand this concern is understandable, for one only needs to look at mainstream Protestant churches, where if a pastor leaves his pastorate without a suitably qualified replacement, an exodus of members may result. This outcome is avoided with the Christadelphian egalitarian model. The cult of person-ality and the problems that accompany a super-star pastor are avoided when no single person is held up above the rest of the community, as is the case with the Christadelphians.

However, on the other hand, the wholesale rejection of the paid ministry model can have unattended negative consequences, since the smaller the denomination is and the less polished and professional it appears to outsiders, the harder it is for the movement to gain credibility and respect and to grow in size. When it comes to matters of theology, Christadelphians are mostly self-taught, eschewing seminaries and aca-demic degrees in theology. Though not always a bad thing, those who choose to follow this model will always struggle against the stereotype that their denomination is little more than an organic, home church movement. Without a growth in numbers at the local level, the children of Christadelphians are prone to reject the primitive sectarianism of their parents, mostly due to limited prospects of marriage within a small faith community.

With respect to baptized Christadelphians, the percentage who leave the community due to a change in their doctrinal beliefs is almost negligible. Even fewer are disfellowshipped on account of unrepentant behavior. But the fact is, some Christadelphians do become ex-Christa-delphians, which only muddies the waters, especially these days when anyone with a computer device can voice their displeasure online and get immediate attention through social media platforms and as a result of search engine algorithms.

Reading what a few disgruntled ex-Christadelphians have posted online, although interesting, does not pass for serious research if that is all that your investigation into the Christadelphians amounts to. Such shallow efforts are more the equivalent of gossip than research. Going no further than pursuing complaints from ex-Christadelphians who hold grudges due to a perceived waste of their childhood within the community at the hands of their parents, or who leave the community as the result of personality conflicts within their local ecclesia, or who eventually reject God, or reject the Bible and its demands on their lives, or who fail to find affirmation for their new LGBTQ identity and who want to gain sympathy by portraying the Christadelphians as out of touch with the times, rigid and unloving, seeking out such information from such sources is not a fair and impartial way to investigate what Christadelphians believe or their history.

Today, the trend is to seek quick answers. As a result, the Internet has become the quick "go-to" source and often becomes the "final word" on just about everything. Consequently, it is common for an investigation—in this case of a relatively unknown religious group, its history and its teachings—to comprise little more than a Google search to see what someone else says. But we must be very careful about accepting what we find on the Internet, and even in books, especially if we always choose sources that agree with our current point of view. There will always be the disgruntled—those who have an ax to grind—along with the zealous heresy hunters, who wish to draw attention to themselves, sometimes with half-truths and one-sided arguments, and whose web pages make it to the top of the search engine algorithms begging to be clicked (see chapter 3). These sites satisfy our tendencies to protect our own tribe and our own position by allowing us to conclude the worst about a group who might pose a threat to our status quo. Because none of us wish to discover that our current "truth" is not really true, we are susceptible to the satisfaction such shallow investigations bring to our penchant to bias, indifference, and lethargy.

Having one's religious beliefs challenged by a small religious group such as the Christadelphians can be an unwanted thing. But let us be fair and not resort to quick and emotional responses and name calling as a way to avoid investigating topics that we as Christians should be taking more seriously.

In conclusion, these pages are the culmination of an encounter not with a cult, but rather with a Christian denomination that does not walk in step with mainstream Christianity. This makes them different, but it doesn't make them a cult. My hope is that I have conducted this investigation of the Christadelphians critically yet fairly, and that my own pursuit for the truth has been done with integrity, determination, and accuracy. It is my hope that the reader will do the same.

Appendix

I F WE SURVEY the various denominations of Christianity, whether they be the well-established ones such as the Roman Catholic Church, the Jehovah's Witnesses, the Seventh-Day Adventists, the Mormons, or even non-denominational groups, we find that these groups often have one feature in common. Though they generally claim to accept the Bible as their ultimate authority, in practice there is a human authority of some kind exalted over the Bible. In some cases it is one person. In the larger and longer-established denominations it is a committee or council. Coupled with this is sometimes the acceptance of other writings which are treated as having the same authority as the Bible, (though in practice they often hold greater authority), as with the *Book of Mormon*, or, in the case of Seventh-Day Adventists, the writings of Ellen White.

As a result of all this, we find that the doctrines held by these groups change over time. This is well documented to be the case with regards to Roman Catholicism, the Jehovah's Witnesses and the Mormons. These changes are not the result of general consensus. The new doctrines which are introduced by them are not the product of a more careful study of Scripture. Instead, they arise because the leadership, whether in the form of a person or a group, decides that a change is needed, for whatever reason.

There is a smaller number of religious groups outside the mainstream which operate on opposite principles. For those groups, such as the Quakers and Unitarian Universalists, there is very little in the way of fixed Christian beliefs. In such groups, individual members can believe virtually anything they wish.

Christadelphians sit between these two extremes. Christadelphians do have firm beliefs, no question; but where they differ from the above mentioned groups is that their beliefs are not decided for them by an individual or committee claiming Divine authority. The authority to which the Christadelphians look is the Bible. What the Christadelphians hold in common among themselves is not the result of an interpretation of Scripture defined by them or by some leader or group who supposedly has or had Divine authority, but rather, the common interpretation comes from taking the Bible at face value, taking proper account of context, history, original languages, figures of speech, literary types, and using the whole Bible, not just parts.

Statements of Faith

It is not possible to readily ascertain when the first statement of faith was formulated and adopted within the Christadelphian community. By the 1870s there were organized ecclesias in various parts of the world, meeting upon a defined basis of faith and with a degree of organization suitable to their size. There is on record one ecclesia in Birmingham, England, which shows that in 1875 they had a statement of faith in two parts: "Truth to be Believed" and "Fables to be Refused."

In 1883, the document known as the *Ecclesial Guide* was first published and distributed widely, in which a set of propositions could be found, entitled, "A Statement of the Doctrines forming the Christadelphian Basis of Fellowship." It is this on which the following summary of Christadelphian beliefs is based.

A Statement of the Doctrines forming the Christadelphian Basis of Fellowship

I. That there is only one true God—He who was revealed to Abraham, Isaac and Jacob and to Moses, the supreme self-existent Deity, the Father, who dwells in unapproachable light, yet is everywhere present, and who has created heaven and earth, and all that is in them. It is this one God who also creates both good and who creates evil/calamity. There is no other G/god beside Him, not on earth or in heaven or in any realm of this universe, nor is there any other eternal being against whom He competes or who opposes His will.

II. That Jesus of Nazareth was the Son of God, born of a virgin named Mary through the miraculous spirit of God, without the intervention of man, and who afterwards was anointed with the same holy spirit, without measure, at his baptism.

III. That the birth of Jesus was necessary due to the position and state into which the human race had been brought by the circumstances connected with the first man.

IV. That the first man was Adam, who God created out of the dust of the ground and declared as "very good" in kind and condition, and placed him under a law through which the continuance of life was contingent on obedience.

V. That Adam broke this law, and was judged unworthy of immortality, and sentenced to return to the ground from whence he was taken. This sentence became a physical law of his being, and was transmitted to all his posterity. Those who descend from Adam follow in the footsteps of the first man when they commit sin, having only themselves to blame for their failure to resist temptation, resulting in their condemnation before God.

VI. That God, in His kindness, conceived a plan of restoration which, without setting aside His just and necessary law of sin and death, should ultimately rescue the race of Adam from sin, death and destruction.

VII. That God inaugurated this plan by making promises in the presence of Adam, Abraham and David, concerning a promised Seed, who would be a savior/redeemer. These promises were afterwards elaborated in greater detail through the prophets.

VIII. That these promises had reference to one who would one day be raised up in the line of Abraham and David, and who, though obedience and by putting to death the desires of his flesh, obtain a title to resurrection. It is through his death that abolished the law of condemnation for himself, who was a representative of mankind, and for all who should believe and obey him.

IX. That it was this mission that necessitated the miraculous birth of Jesus of a human mother, enabling him to bear our condemnation, and, at the same time, to be a sinless bearer thereof, and, therefore, one who could rise back to life after suffering the death required by the righteousness of God.

X. That being so born of God, and being led by the indwelling of God's spirit and by His teachings and divine laws, Jesus could be deemed as having been "sent by God," and in a greater sense as "Emmanuel"—God with us—serving as God's representative agent and mouthpiece to mankind.

XI. That the message that Jesus delivered from God to his kinsmen, the Jews, was a call to repentance from every evil work, the acknowledgment of his divine "sonship"—a reference to Jewish kingship—and the proclamation of the good news (gospel) that God would restore the former rule over their nation through him, and accomplish all things written in the prophets concerning this restoration.

XII. That for delivering this message, Jesus was put to death by the Jews and Romans who were, however, but instruments in the hands of God, for the doing of that which He had preordain from the beginning of time to be done, viz., the condemnation of sin through the offering of the body of Jesus once for all, as a sin-covering to declare the righteousness of God, as a basis for the remission of sins. All who approach God through this crucified, but risen, representative of Adam's disobedient race, are forgiven. Therefore, by a figure, his blood cleanses from sin.

XIII. That on the third day after his death, God raised him from the dead, and exalted him as the one and only priestly mediator between God and mankind, and in the process gathering from among the nations a people who should be saved.

XIV. That Jesus as a priest, makes intercession for his erring brothers and sisters in this faith, if they confess and forsake their sins.

XV. That Jesus sent forth apostles to proclaim salvation through him, as the only Name given under heaven whereby men and women may be saved.

XVI. That the way to obtain this salvation is to believe the gospel they preached, and to take on the name and service of Christ, by being thereupon baptized (immersed in water), and continuing patiently in the observance of all things he has commanded.

XVII. That the gospel consists of "the things concerning the kingdom of God and the name of Jesus Christ."

XVIII. That the things of the Kingdom of God are the facts testified concerning the Kingdom of God in the writings of the prophets and apostles, and definable as in the next 12 paragraphs.

XIX. That God will set up a kingdom on the earth, which will overthrow all others, and change them into "the kingdoms of our Lord and His Anointed." (Revelation 11:15)

XX. That for this purpose God will send Jesus personally to the earth at the close of the times of the Gentiles.

XXI. That the kingdom which he will establish will be the kingdom of Israel restored, in the territory it formerly occupied, viz., the land bequeathed for an everlasting possession to Abraham and his seed (the Messiah) by covenant. (Genesis 13:17, 17:8; Galatians 3:16)

XXII. That this restoration of the kingdom again to Israel will involve the ingathering of God's chosen but scattered nation, the Jews; their reinstatement in the land of their fathers, when it shall have been reclaimed from "the desolation of many generations;" the building again of Jerusalem to become "the throne of the LORD" and the "city of the great king."

XXIII. That the governing body of the Kingdom so established will be the brethren of Christ, of all generations, developed by resurrection and change, and constituting, with Christ as their head, the collective "seed of Abraham," in whom all nations will be blessed, and comprising "Abraham, Isaac, and Jacob, and all the prophets," and all in their age of like faithfulness.

XXIV. That a law will be established, which shall go forth to the nations for their "instruction in righteousness," resulting in the abolition of war to the ends of the earth; and the "filling of the earth with the knowledge of the glory of God, as the waters cover the sea."

XXV. That at the appearing of Christ prior to the establishment of the Kingdom, the responsible (faithful and unfaithful), dead and living of both classes, will be summoned before his judgment-seat "to be judged according to their works;" "and receive in body according to what they have done, whether it be good or bad."

XXVI. That the unfaithful will be consigned to shame and "the second death," which involves an eventual and final cessation of all life, while the faithful, bestowed with immortality, are exalted to reign with Jesus as joint heirs of the Kingdom, and will be co-possessors of the earth, and joint administrators of God's authority among men in everything.

XXVII. That the Kingdom of God, thus constituted, will continue a thousand years, during which sin and death will continue among the earth's subject-inhabitants, though in a much milder degree than now.

XXVIII. That the mission of the Kingdom will be to subdue all enemies, and finally death itself, by opening up the way of life to the nations, which they will enter by faith, during the thousand years, and (in reality) at their close.

XXIX. That at the close of the thousand years, there will be a general resurrection and judgment, resulting in the final extinction of the wicked, and the immortalization of those who shall have established their title (under the grace of God) to eternal life during the thousand years.

XXX. That the government will then be delivered up by Jesus to the Father, who will manifest Himself as the "All-in-all;" sin and death having been taken out of the way, and the race completely restored to the friendship of the God.

XXXI. That the Scriptures, composing the book currently known as the Bible, are the only source now available of knowledge concerning God and His purposes.

Made in United States
Troutdale, OR
08/29/2023

12462495R00120